THE
GAWKER
GUIDE TO
CONQUERING
ALL MEDIA

THE
GAWKER
GUIDE TO

CONQUERING ALL MEDIA

GAWKER MEDIA

Written by **CHELSEA PERETTI** and **BRIDIE CLARK**

With contributions by Mike Albo, Fred Armisen, Jackie Clarke, Brian Donovan, Emily Gould, Jim Hanas, Laura Krafft, Todd Levin, Amanda Melson, A.D. Miles, Abdi Nazemian, Jim Norton, Bob Powers, Nic Rapold, Andrea Rosen, Michael Showalter, and Kate Spencer

Produced by **GABY DARBYSHIRE**

ATRIA BOOKS

New York   London   Toronto   Sydney

ATRIA BOOKS

A Division of Simon & Schuster, Inc.
1230 Avenue of the Americas
New York, NY 10020

First Atria Books hardcover edition October 2007

ATRIA BOOKS and colophon are trademarks of Simon & Schuster, Inc.

For information about special discounts for bulk purchases, please contact
Simon & Schuster Special Sales at 1-800-456-6798
or business@simonandschuster.com.

Designed by Joel Avirom and Jason Snyder
Design assistant: Meghan Day Healey
Illustrations by Jason Snyder

Manufactured in the United States of America

1 3 5 7 9 10 8 6 4 2

Library of Congress Cataloging-in-Publication Data
The gawker guide to conquering all media / by Gawker Media.
p. cm.
1. Mass media—Humor. I. Gawker Media.
PN6231.M33G39 2007
302.2302'07—dc22
2007010161

ISBN-13: 978-1-4165-3299-6
ISBN-10:   1-4165-3299-4

CONTENTS

INTRODUCTION IX

1 THE BASICS 1

2 BOOK PUBLISHING 25

3 PRINT 55

4 RADIO 79

5 TV AND FILM 97

6 THE INTERNET 127

7 FINAL PREPARATIONS 157

FURTHER RESOURCES 173

ACKNOWLEDGMENTS 175

THE

GAWKER

GUIDE TO

CONQUERING
ALL MEDIA

INTRODUCTION

POWER. PRESTIGE. RESPECT. MONEY. INFLUENCE. You've got some but want more, much more. You sell books, appear in magazines, own buildings, sponsor awards, chair committees, and dictate the Top Ten of everything that matters (movies, restaurants, models), but it's not enough. You want to be known for your haircut. You want everything you touch to make money and to be getting laid more than Dave Zinczenko. Who cares if you're going to have to pay dearly for it?

You know the successful never rest. You know the media landscape is forever shifting, and one must be equally shifty in order to stay on top. We're here to foist you upwards with our strong, gentle hands. Welcome to Gawker in print.

That's right, Gawker offline: no scrolling, no internet connectivity required. A book filled with hard-won wisdom from years of observing, reporting on, and occasionally stalking the rich and powerful. Do you remember how to hold a book? We know you can do it. And if you do . . . you shall be richly rewarded.

Because what we're about to reveal will change your life.

Other career guides tell you that keeping your nose to the grindstone will help you reach the pinnacle of success. We believe in shortcuts.

Before we illuminate every nook and cranny of the media, a few promises:

✓ Yes! This book provides definitive information.

✓ Yes! This book will make you better.

✓ Um-hm! Reading this book instantly fixes anything that feels "broken" in you.

✓ Imagine that *über*-success waits for you behind a big door in the topmost room of your house. You know that topmost room belongs to you, yet you can't figure out how to access it. This book is the key that will unlock that door. Hope you like mediocre metaphorical visualizations!

Ever look at all you've achieved and feel like a worthless piece of shit inside because at the end of the day you're still not God? You're not alone, friend. The good news is that this book will bring you closer to being God. Not closer in an "I pray" way, but closer in a Jay-Z, everyone-is-humbled-when-you-enter-the-room type way.

You can't do it without us. We provide the answers you've been searching for all your life, in meeting after meeting, auction after auction, premiere after premiere, opening after opening, press function after press function, gala fund-raiser after gala fund-raiser. We provide the outline for a lifetime of A+ performances.

So tonight, turn your back on your lover, spouse, or that perpetually empty side of your king-sized imported Italian-linen designer bed, and curl towards this book instead. For between its covers lies all you have ever wanted.

Cancel that visit to your grandmother—she isn't that sick, and she's not a key priority.

Ixnay on the iptray to the countryside with a group of your closest friends—you know your career can't wait. Ever. And that everything else can. Forever.

If one day you're successful to the point where your pills and personal staff are the closest friends you have, congrats. This book has served you well, and we've done our job.

Go forth ye lonely, greedy soul! There is media, waiting to be conquered.

GLOSSARY OF ICONS

As with all top career guides, our book is punctuated with helpful icons. But it gets better. At Gawker, we are pleased to feature more icons than any other existing guide on the market. Our icon catalogue contains not two, not three, but thirteen distinct icons! Look for them everywhere your eye rests on every page.

 Pay attention, this is an important point!

 Power check.

 Stop. Read this section to make sure you got it.

 Kiss-up tip.

 Inspirational wisdom.

 Make a note of this in pencil. It's good, but not our best advice ever.

 Make a note of this in pen. It *is* our best advice ever.

 What to wear tip.

 Make more money tip.

 DIY tip.

 Think outside the box.

 You might want to skip this section. It's useless. We started to drink heavily as the book deadline approached.

 Sidestep suggestion.

PERSONALITY TYPE: WHERE DO YOU BELONG?

This is a worksheet for you to fill in, so that you may better understand the general career path fit to your particular strengths. Look at each question below, look within yourself, and write down your preferences.

Please circle one:

Do you prefer to fetch an iced cappuccino OR have someone fetch it for you?

Why:

_____

_____

_____

Do you prefer to pick up your dry cleaning OR have someone pick that up for you?

Why:

_____

_____

_____

Cigarettes. Do you enjoy physically going to the store for them OR having another person take this trip and return with your favored brand in tow?

Why:

_____

_____

_____

Do you prefer a shared bathroom (multiple stalls) OR a private bathroom environment?

Why: _____

_____

_____

If you could take your pick between a small desk area in an open space full of indistinguishable desk areas OR an enclosed, private office with a closing door and possible oak paneling—where would you place yourself?

Why: _____

_____

_____

Do you prefer high-end furniture or "whatever's clever"?

Why: _____

_____

_____

Good job! Review what you've written in response to the questions above. You may learn something about your own disposition. For example, if you tend to like to fetch things, you may be better suited to an **executive assistant** career, whereas if you prefer to be tended to, you might look into being a **CEO** or **executive.**

1 THE BASICS

THROUGHOUT TIME, innumerable people have been conquered. Conquerors, on the other hand, have been merely numerable. The cunning media conqueror knows his history well, and turns to the past for inspiration.

THE MORE THINGS CHANGE, THE MORE THEY STAY THE SAME

Ancient Conquerors	Media Elite
Invasion of Roman Empire.	Invasion of Condé Nast.
Occupation of enormous palace.	Occupation of prime table at Michael's.
Overthrow of a previously existing system or regime in neighboring territory.	Overthrow of previous masthead.
Suppression of slave rebellion.	Suppression of assistant's personality.
Merciless tyrant.	"Climber."
Massacre of tens of thousands of people.	Massacre of tens of thousands of packs of cigarettes.
Defeat at the hands of a rival conqueror.	Defeat of ever paying for drinks.
Victory in long, bloody battle.	Victory in long quotation battle on Page Six.
Assassination of competitive younger brother.	Assassination of own conscience.
Mastery of raping and pillaging.	Same.

Today's media conqueror must be constantly poised for battle. Let's do a quick check on your arsenal. Do your emails have a glaring subtext of superiority? Do you know how to exploit personal relationships for business gain? Read on.

INVESTIGATIVE BANTER: HOW TO GRILL A PROFESSIONAL FRIEND MERCILESSLY IN THE GUISE OF A "HANG"

No matter which branch of the media you work in, investigative banter is a vital job skill. Perfect it or quit the game. Remember: If your inquiries *sound* polite, your companion will probably feel compelled to answer.

As your companion unknowingly babbles, take careful notes below on anything that might prove incriminating/useful.

SAMPLE INVESTIGATIVE BANTER:

Are you still working at X?

_____

_____

_____

No?! (shocked pause, eliciting further detail)

_____

_____

_____

Why not, what happened?

_____

_____

_____

Ooh! So then who hired you for your current gig?

_____

_____

_____

How'd you find out about it?

_____

_____

_____

Isn't so and so mad about that? I would be!

_____

_____

_____

Is the pay okay?

_____

_____

_____

Are you working closely with anyone else?

_____

_____

_____

Is s/he any good?

_____

_____

_____

CAREFUL! ASK AND YE SHALL PROBABLY RECEIVE . . .

I f you're dealing out the questions, chances are your opponent will fire back. When you find yourself on the *receiving* end of "friendly" interrogation, make like a crab and sidestep.

Take the previous example question: "Is the pay good?"

A quick sidestep turns the question back:

"I'm not sure! Salaries are so relative—what do you make?"

Or try a rhetorical sidestep:

"Ain't pay always good?"

Or an evasive adage/exclamation:

"Well, the early bird gets the worm, I can tell you that much!"

Then ask for the check and jump in a cab . . . it's like you were never there.

> If you want to be a big gun, you've got to start thinking of yourself as a big gun: alternatively silent and explosive . . . cold . . . evil. Or think of yourself as a remote island, or a castle surrounded by a moat full of crocodiles, or a big vat of shit or something else no human would want to be near.

THE PROFESSIONAL FRIENDSHIP

There are many subtle emotional boundaries in the workplace. *Office romance* is frowned upon, yet *camaraderie* is encouraged. Navigating this subtle terrain can be confounding, even for the top executive.

Professional friendships are often confusing. They can lead to such unanswered questions as:

"Why has my co-worker been avoiding me ever since I made her a friendship bracelet?"

Well, for starters, your office staff isn't your high school clique—it's a team of disloyal, backstabbing undercover agents. Okay, so, it's very much *like* your high school clique. But once an annual salary is involved, particular rules of conduct apply.

Behavior	Professional Friends	Personal Friends
Tell sad story about your father	NO	YES
Name-drop powerful people that you know	YES	YES
Grab cocktails at T.G.I. Friday's the moment work is done	NO	NO
Provide occasional sex	YES	YES
Tell calculated anecdotes designed to highlight your strengths	YES	YES
French braid their hair at a slumber party	YES	YES

Never mind, there isn't much difference. Just don't tell people at work that story about your father. At a certain point, you might think they're ready—but they'll never be ready.

STUPID QUESTIONS

Over the years, you've no doubt been told that there's no such thing as a stupid question. Unfortunately, this is a ridiculous falsehood.

*Stupid questions do exist. They are **real**. There are many of them. And they can destroy you.*

Here are some stupid questions to avoid during a key job interview.

- Do you mind if I eat my lunch while you talk?

- Could you guesstimate how long it would take me to advance to your exact position?

- Do these pants make my ass look big? Be completely fucking honest!!!

- Let's see if you read my résumé. What was I doing between . . . '95 and '96?

- How strict is the company's firewall when it comes to artistic portrayals of children's sexuality?

- Your assistant seems unhappy. Any idea why?

THE PROFESSIONAL THANK YOU

Email is a common format for the contemporary thank-you message (e.g., "Thanks again for lunch. Let's follow up soon on my tab"). However, when you want to go the extra mile, a hard copy—or "thank you note"—is your best bet.

Fold a sheet of heavy stock paper (preferably high gloss) in two to create a Hallmark-caliber greeting card for business use. Have fun with this craft.

Here are a few bon mots to inspire you.

YOU UNDERSTAND ME . . .

ON A BUSINESS LEVEL.

THANK YOU AGAIN!

FOR COVERING
MY TRAVEL COSTS.

YOU'VE NEVER
SEXUALLY
HARASSED ME.

THANK YOU,
I APPRECIATE
THAT WORK
ENVIRONMENT.

YOUR WIFE WAS ALL OVER ME AT THE COMPANY PICNIC!

THANKS FOR MAKING THAT POSSIBLE.

THANK YOU . . .

FOR SPEAKING AT OUR CONFERENCE. I HEARD YOU WERE STRONG.

NAME-DROPPING

How many names do you know: a thousand? Two thousand? Six? Who you know is everything in the media biz. Second in importance is letting others know who you know. Name-dropping is an art form that can take years to perfect, but following these basic rules will get you off to a good start.

Rule #1: Keep it subtle, especially when dropping A-list names.

If the person is truly famous, never overtly say that you know them, you've spoken to them, or they're a friend. That's tacky. Instead, gracefully weave in a mention of something they said—an opinion, a witticism, a penchant for a certain kind of Camembert. (Example: "That's a scream, Denzel was just going on and on about Le Châtelain.")

Rule #2: If you have to ask, you're a loser.

Never explain the identity of your dropped name. If the person you're talking to doesn't know who Len Riggio is, that's their problem and your cool point.

Rule #3: Fake it till you make it.

Nine times out of ten, your listeners won't admit to not knowing who someone is—they'll act blasé and pretend they do. This is a loophole you want to exploit. It means that any name—famous, successful, or not—can be dropped without questioning. (Note: The more pretentious and British-sounding the name, the less likely you'll be asked to explain who the person is).

DROP IT LIKE IT'S HOT

Need to drop a name, but have no connection to a name worth dropping? Mix 'n' match names from various branches of the media, and you'll end up with something formidable. Go ahead, bluff it up!

LEONARDO DICAPRIO
+ ANDERSON COOPER
= ANDERSON DICAPRIO

"Anderson DiCaprio tells the *most* hilarious penguin story . . ."

BARBARA WALTERS
+ BINKY URBAN
= BINKY WALTERS

"Hmm . . . I'm meeting Binky Walters at the Soho House in ten, so let me get back to you on that."

M. NIGHT SHYAMALAN
+ MORGAN ENTREKIN
= M. NIGHT ENTREKIN

"M. Night Entrekin just invited me to join his table, so I'll probably be there . . ."

ENTER THE OFFICE

Every media conqueror has an HQ that reflects his or her powerful stature, insatiable ambition, and general ass-kicking nature. Is it time for you to upgrade? Take a look around your office. What is that generic Ansel Adams photograph telling visitors about *you*? That you like trees? Not good enough.

Display art that's phallic instead—a skyscraper, a missile launch, a cobra, a cucumber and a heavy pair of tomatoes. Let all your visitors know: Big Kahuna isn't just a ridiculous nickname—it's a ridiculous way of life.

1   Media conquerors get away with shit. Whether it's Graydon Carter chain-smoking in his office or Scott Rudin flogging his assistants for hours on end, you haven't *really* made it until you can piss in the face of office etiquette.

   To that end, why not resurrect the fully stocked office bar? Crystal decanter, martini shaker, jumbo olives, silver stirrers . . . and you're ready for a quick nip. It's not just your midday drunkenness that will impress colleagues, but the fact that you can get away with it.

2   Keep celeb pictures on the shelves. Bonus: celebs recognized by first name only.

3   Become the office dealer. Stock up on mints, cologne, Viagra, and cigars, and casually make it clear to co-workers that you have what they need when they need it.

4   The computer might well be the most important invention of our century, revolutionizing the very way we think about thinking, viewing porn, and blogging. Computers are as vital to today's communication as the wing-footed messenger was to the ancient Greeks.

   That's exactly why *not* having one is so bold. Not owning a personal computer makes a ballsy announcement to the world: "The computer is something my assistant touches, while I handle the money."

   Your assistant prints out all your incoming email, hand delivers to you. Then you pull out your Montblanc, jot some quick thoughts on the top of the page ("let's discuss" or "no" underlined thrice, two excellent note choices), and hand back to your assistant, who does the rest.

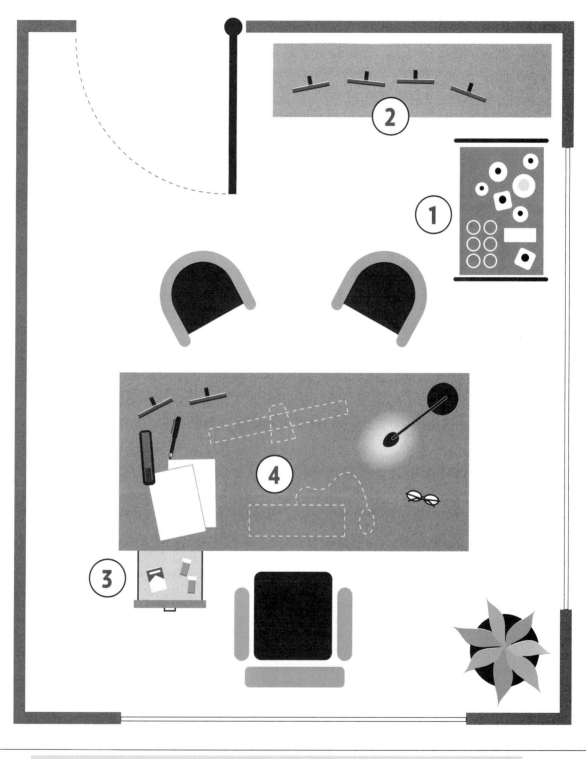

POWER ASSESSMENT

Ever idly think: "I know I'm powerful, but I wonder *how powerful?*" while munching crudités on a 360-degree view balcony, bidding on a limited edition piece of art, or experiencing release at a high-end massage parlor?

How do you assess and quantify your own power? There are many techniques. Some involve mountaintops and shouting into the skies. Less mystical options discussed below.

BODY LANGUAGE

Over the next few days, pay attention to the physical "language" spoken by the people who surround you.

When you speak to other professionals, do they:

Fold their arms across their chests?	Y N
Close their eyes for lengthy periods of time, as if trying to erase something?	Y N
Cover their ears?	Y N
Swivel in chair, in order to face away from you?	Y N
Text, email, or "surf the net"?	Y N
Make remarks such as: "Ooohh! I wish I were playing with a puppy right now!"	Y N

If you answered "Y" to any of the previous questions, you're about as powerful as a 50-watt bulb. Using strategies delineated in this book, pay close attention and try to shift the physical response of your professional contacts to the following:

- Nervousness, not sure what to do with hands.

- Eyebrows raised frequently in "eyebrow interest pose."

- Nodding, nodding, nodding . . . nodding . . . nodding . . . nodding . . .

- Hair-trigger laughter response. Laughing, laughing . . . (Seems like nothing could be that funny. It isn't. You're powerful!)

- Note taking.

- Child's pose (yoga position, see diagram below).

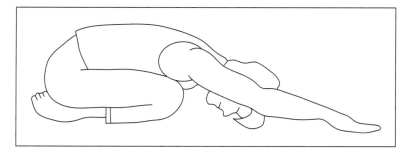

Facially, they should resemble a brainwashed cult member: beatific, eyes glossed, smiling, optimistic. The cult is you.

PHONE ETIQUETTE: ANSWERING THE PHONE

 Each phone call is an elaborate theatrical production and an opportunity to tell the world that you're in control of your game.

When the phone rings,

Do	Don't
Glance at caller ID screen. If caller is important, scowl and answer yourself. Or instruct your assistant to ask who's calling and then to immediately relay that you're in a meeting.	Recite the name of the company you work for in your greeting.
Murmur a guess about who might be calling ("Probably Sonny Mehta").	Use phrases such as "good morning," "good afternoon," "good evening," or "how may I help you?"
Affect a busy, distracted tone of voice.	Have any "smile" in your voice.

All conversations should end abruptly with "okay, gotta jump."

When placing calls, all conversations should begin without a greeting. Dive into the heart of the matter without stating your name. Everyone should know who you are by the sound of your voice.

SAMPLE DIALOGUE

[Phone rings.]

ASSISTANT: "Ari Emanuel's office, can I help you?"

YOU: "You read Friedman's editorial this morning?"

ASSISTANT: "I'm sorry, who may I—"

YOU: "Genius. Let's get something started there. The timing is perfect, am I right?"

ASSISTANT: "Is this Michael? *[uncertain pause]* Tom?"

YOU: "Is the big guy free?"

ASSISTANT: "He's in a meeting—"

YOU: "Tell him to call me asap on this one. Ciao."

ASSISTANT: "Wait, I don't—"

Don't worry about the fact that you've left no contact information. The assistant will find you. What do you think she's paid $20k a year for, filling candy jars?

YOU READ THIS SOMEWHERE

*"Sarcasm is the lowest form of humor." FALSE.
Doo-doo humor is lower. And the form where you
think it's funny to spit on someone in their face.*

RSVP STRATEGY: A COST-BENEFIT ANALYSIS

Some people choose after-work activities based on their passions and interests. We refer to these people as "drain circlers."

In the media world, you must constantly weigh the value of "showing up." You must evaluate stakes: What will the face time do for your career? How can you get the most while giving the least? How elite is the event and what's the boldface potential of other attendees? Consult the chart below for help with your future event analysis.

Event	Pros	Cons	Bottom Line
Book Signing	Brief, relatively painless.	No booze, fluorescent lighting.	Only attend if you're signing books.
Magazine Launch Party	Unfiltered access to drunken EICs, who—away from the paternal gaze of their managing editors—might accidentally expose a chink in their armor that will help you usurp their positions.	The magazine won't be around in sixty days.	Press-hungry celebs likely to attend. Arrive early (i.e., two hours late) and hang with mag staffers. It's their big night, following several stressful months of struggling to bring their vision to the page. They'll lap up praise and be putty in your hands. And have expensive drugs.

Event	Pros	Cons	Bottom Line
Award Show	Spectacular open bars.	Interminable speechifying.	Good star spotting and free drinks. Bring a friend with whom you want to curry favor.
Charity Benefit	A great way to showcase your "selfless side" to peers. Good philanthropist poaching: meet people with money to burn (investors, venture capitalists, heiresses).	None of the A-listers advertised on the invitation will be there.	If there is a silent auction, bid early and often—look like a big roller while safe in the knowledge that you will be outbid.

"YOU'RE INVITED!" NETWORKING POP QUIZ

What's the difference between a cocktail party, a tête-à-tête, a gathering, a soiree, and a rendezvous? If someone invites you to one, you certainly don't want to show up dressed for the other. Make your best guess and mail to the address at right:

PLACE
STAMP
HERE

GAWKER MEDIA
DO NOT RESPOND DIVISION
555 SOHO LANE
NY, NY 00000

SELF-EVALUATION: ARE YOU AT THE TOP OF YOUR GAME AS A PERSON AND CAREER PROFESSIONAL?

Evaluate your personality by placing an "X" in the appropriate box. Is your personality "perfect" in a given category or could it possibly "improve"?

My Personality	Perfect	Could Improve
WIT	☐	☐
ORIGINALITY	☐	☐
CHARISMA	☐	☐
STYLE	☐	☐
HUMILITY IN MOMENTS OF SELF-EVALUATION	☐	☐
PERFECTION	☐	☐

YOU READ THIS SOMEWHERE

Excel spreadsheets and Quicken software are equally helpful at minimizing one's fear of death.

Answer Key

My Personality	Perfect	Could Improve
WIT	☒	☐
ORIGINALITY	☒	☐
CHARISMA	☒	☐
STYLE	☒	☐
HUMILITY IN MOMENTS OF SELF-EVALUATION	☒	☐
PERFECTION	☒	☐

If you marked that you were "perfect" in every category, you're ready to succeed. In today's job market, that's the correct way to think—and it's contagious. So get out there and edge out the competition. They may *be* more qualified than you, but you *be-lieve* you're more qualified. And that's all that matters.

Carefully cut this out and glue it to the front of your computer monitor:

MY CONFIDENCE IS MY QUALIFICATION!

FIRST STEPS

Now that we've covered the basics, let's decide which branch of media you should dominate first. This quiz will help illuminate your career path:

1   Of all the branches of media, do you enjoy **book publishing** most?

2   Do you like **magazine** and **print journalism** best?

3   Or **television** and **film?**

4   Do you prefer the **internet?**

5   Is **radio** your favorite?

Answer key: If you answered yes to question 1, you should tackle book publishing first. If you answered yes to question 2, magazine and print journalism will be your first attack. If yes to question 3, head to television and film. If yes 4, internet. If 5, radio.

2 BOOK PUBLISHING

WELCOME TO BOOK PUBLISHING, an old-school branch of the media known for low salaries.

HOW DOES THE BOOK PUBLISHING INDUSTRY REALLY WORK?

Great question! It doesn't really work. But the good news is that the industry's ass-backwardness makes it an easy mark for domination. Virtually anyone can become a bestselling author, a leading editor, or a book publisher. All it takes is basic literacy and a few decades of free time.

EDITORS: HOW TO SPOT A FUTURE BESTSELLER

Snickering over that 700-page submission about a Roman centurion vampire who had a gay affair with Jesus Christ? Well, instead of Xeroxing the first few pages to pass around for giggles at the ed meeting, maybe you should be putting it up for acquisition. These days, it's becoming harder and harder to tell "crap" from "the kind of crap that sells hundreds of thousands of copies."

YOU SHOULD BUY IT IF . . .

1 Your first concern is "Are we sure the target audience for this is actually, you know, literate?"

2 Your first concern is "Are we sure that the celebrity 'author' is actually, you know, literate?"

3 The title fits this template: The _____ [intriguing compound noun]'s _____ [daughter, wife, or mother]. Book clubs are preordering it already and we haven't even filled in the blanks.

4 The plot involves the Bible/the Masons/any old secret society, really— and some kind of cryptological twist. Yes, still.

5 The mere thought of having anything to do with the conservative-pundit author makes you want to run screaming from the room and take four hundred consecutive showers.

6 The celebrity "author" seems likely to die or be convicted of a felony within the coming year (but not before signing off on everything).

7 It's a "harrowing" memoir ("harrowing" = lots of puking scenes, basically). Yes, still.

8 It's a lifestyle guide by a celebrity whose lifestyle is worth emulating . . . if your idea of a life goal is to be "#1 in upskirt photos on the internet."

9 It's a catchily titled, easily digestible novel or memoir about an area of the world that's in the news a lot (e.g., Afghanistan, Tehran). People will snap it up like the liberal-guilt-assuaging vitamin that it is, no matter how purple the prose.

10 It's a novel about an average-looking middle-aged lady who somehow ends up with money, babies, romance, or fame (ideally all four).

There you go. You now have the instincts of Judith Regan, but you bypassed the whole messy selling-your-soul-to-Satan part.

EDITORS: REJECTING YOUR WAY TO SUCCESS

Central to the editor's job is the art of a diplomatic rejection letter. The rejection letter provides a public record of the fact that you received the proposal and passed. It finesses a cold "no" for the agent and author, praising them just enough to save their fragile egos. Even if the submission was a steaming pile of crap, a well-worded rejection letter makes the agent feel like you still respect him professionally—which keeps you in the running should he ever end up representing anything halfway decent.

AN EDITOR'S GUIDE TO ADJECTIVES

The euphemistic adjective is an editor's best friend. Here's a few to keep on hand:

"lyrical" = sappy, faux poetic, containing too many superfluous SAT vocab words.

"haunting" = I tried to make myself forget I had ever read a single word of this, but it was too disturbingly bad.

"provocative" = it made me really hate the author.

"raw" = clearly a cry for psychological help.

"a lot of heart" = vomitously sweet.

"fascinating" = not fascinating.

"smart" = I'll throw you a meaningless bone.

SAMPLE LETTERS

Let's take a closer look at some rejection letters.

THE REMAINDER PRESS
222 MIDTOWN AVENUE
NEW YORK, NY 00000

small-time agent

Dear _____,

I want to thank you for the chance to consider *I'm a Rich Urban Mom Still Trying to Be Hot* by A. Not-so-famousmagazinewriter. I found the story both wonderfully honest and funny, and believe that this novel would make a great addition to the chick-lit/mommy-lit genre.

This had moments of non-terribleness, but the author has hopped on the mommy-lit bandwagon way too late—duh!

Unfortunately, though, we do so little fiction here that in order to take on a novel I have to believe it has exceptional frontlist upside. In this case, I see the book more as a great addition to an established women's fiction list. So without the vision for it, I'm not going to be able to take it on.

Trying to sound profesh by flinging jargon around! Duck!

This is a perfect excuse because it has nothing whatsoever to do with the book. A good rejection is like a bad breakup: it's not you, it's me!

agent who persists in sending lame-ass "literary" fiction and is obviously unfamiliar with the editor's list →

"this bizarre, possibly racist crap"

Dear _____,

"I have no clue what could possibly have motivated anyone to write"

Thank you so much for the chance to read *Mubuntu's Magical-Realistic Adventures as Portrayed Semi-offensively* by A. Whiteperson. I loved the idea behind this quirky novel, but in the end, I'm afraid, I just didn't find Mubuntu that compelling as a main character. We do so little fiction here that I'm really not able to get our team behind a novel unless I'm truly in love with it myself, and I just wasn't quite there. So, I'll have to step aside. ←

This is the tried-and-true "completely arbitrary reason grabbed from a hat," often found preceded by "but in the end" or "ultimately."

Yeah, not quite.

"I would never in a million years have dreamed of inflicting this read on my colleagues— I even felt bad forcing it on the intern."

What grace and diplomacy! How big of you to "step aside"! If this were a breakup, you'd be saying, "You deserve someone who can give you what I can't."

THE REMAINDER PRESS
222 MIDTOWN AVENUE
NEW YORK, NY 00000

older, respected agent whom we can't risk offending

Dear _____,

"I was so intrigued," "found this fascinating" fall under the same category as expressions like "long story short" and "no offense but." Opposite day!

Thank you so much for sending the proposal for *Daddy's Hands, Mommy's Heart, Children's Memories* by Sappy McSicklysweet. I was so intrigued by the concept here and I found the author's voice enchanting, but I ultimately worried that we just wouldn't know how to go about getting this the publicity and distribution that it would need. I am sorry to have to pass, but I appreciate the look. I wish you and the author the best of luck.

enchanting = "lyrical"

Another catchall, and it's good because it's at once impersonal and true. Ed assistants' fingers are callused from typing this exact phrase over and over.

See? Other than the basic structure (profuse thanks, faint praise, deep regret, vague but airtight excuse for passing, thanks again) the only things that really change are the adjectives. Keep yourself awake by replacing "gripping" with "riveting" every so often.

Even better, get your assistant to crank these things out for you.

IT'S A JUNGLE OUT THERE

If there's one thing that has been proven by countless highly credentialed career advisors, it's the importance of psychologically identifying with an animal in the workplace.

Let's check in with you and your mind state . . . are you ready to fuck shit up?

Look at the pairings below and select the animal with which you most identify:

1   **(A)** ANTEATER   **(B)** ANT

2   **(A)** CAT   **(B)** MOUSE

3   **(A)** SNAKE   **(B)** MOUSE

4   **(A)** OWL   **(B)** MOUSE

5   **(A)** ALLIGATOR   **(B)** CHICKEN WITH A BROKEN LEG, RESTING BESIDE THE RIVERBANK.

6   **(A)** LION   **(B)** MOUSE

ANSWER KEY

All A's. Snort a little blow and dance in a jerky circle to celebrate—because you're an A-type personality! You've got a proverbial set of balls in your hand at all times, for whenever you're inclined to give a yank.

Single "B" Answer. If you answered "b" only once, fair enough. You were probably enjoying some quirky philosophical approach to the question. Still, keep an eye on yourself . . . you could turn out to be a bit of a doormat.

All "B" Answers. Unacceptable. If you answered B more than once, you're a complete piece of turd. Start striving for an A-type personality pronto or you'll be trading limp handshakes with a pathetic gang of nobodies for the rest of your abysmal career.

"5B" Selected. Do your mom a favor and move out of her basement before it floods and she has to replace your crappy furniture.

YARDSTICK OF AUTHORLY ACHIEVEMENT

Authors are sensitive spirits. As an editor, you'll often be called upon to rally an author's morale when various parts of the publication process don't measure up to his or her expectations. Here are some techniques that'll keep your authors peppy and productive.

What Author Expects	Reality	You Console By . . .
Huge advance after heated bidding war.	Advance is barely enough to live off of—*before* taxes and agent's commission.	Picking up the tab at Burger Heaven.
Massive advance buzz.	The publisher has not found time to read the manuscript.	Another burger at Burger Heaven. Vague talk of "buzz."
Book gets selected for Oprah's Book Club.	50 percent off bin at Barnes & Noble.	Sending author birthday e-card.
20-city book tour.	0-city book tour.	Telling author that book tours are for publicity whores like Ann Coulter—real writers stay home and write.
Second book deal.	First book goes out of print. Author's name, poison.	Consolation difficult since you've cut off all contact.

YOU READ THIS SOMEWHERE

A book cover contains the title, author name, a brief description of the book, praise from other authors, and quick reviews. It's a helpful way to judge a book.

AUTHORS: UNDERSTANDING YOUR BASTARD AGENT

A good agent is well versed in the diplomatic blow-off, the graceful sidestep, and the optimistic non-promise. It's important to understand your agent's unique babble.

What Your Agent Says	What Your Agent Means
"I'm waiting for people to call me back."	"Your book is dead in the water."
"The editor had some hesitations about your proposal."	"Your book is dead in the water."
"Sorry I haven't called you back in two weeks, I've been crazy busy."	"You mean nothing to me. Please lose this number."
"I'll fight for this, but I think it'll be difficult."	"The way I 'fight' is by working on deals for other, more promising talent."
"I'll send your manuscript out one more time . . ."	"I'll send it out to my little sister, who's interning at Knopf this summer. I'll also tell her she doesn't need to read it. I have to charge you for the shipping."
"I read your manuscript and thought it had some great moments— but I think we need to focus on revisions before sending it out."	"Open your document, select *all*, and then hit delete."
"The book seems a little small."	"You might want to see if Kinko's is hiring."
"The feeling is that this book has been done before."	"Tell me, what would draw a person incapable of original thought towards a writing career?"
"Everyone is really excited about your book."	(No meaning.)
"It sounds like they're really going to push your book."	(Again, empty words that translate to nothingness.)
"Any thoughts on what you'd like to write next?"	"My wife wants the kid to go to private school. Don't be lazy."

*Malcolm Gladwell**

So, you've made it. Unfortunately, money doesn't solve everything. And neither does acclaim, and neither does a permanent place in history. Certain problems can still arise. Such as: say your waiter is going through a detailed recitation of the evening's specials and most of them involve a reduction sauce of some sort or another and you despise reduction sauces. Are you required to listen through each special anyways? Or, another problem: How do you gauge what amount of money is appropriate for a book advance after a certain point, when you've begun to lose all sense of proportion?

Being an overwhelming success, a public thinker, a great mind of the twenty-first century, etc., etc., entails a certain amount of "waking pressure," meaning what it takes for me to wake up knowing all that I mean to society is beyond your most extreme imagination. I am a great intellectual and a two-time #1 bestselling author. I am unlike any other author who has ever lived. When I say jump, publishers say: "But Mr. Gladwell, HOW HIGH WOULD YOU LIKE US TO JUMP?" and then they throw suitcases full of money at me and start jumping till I say "Quit it, you guys."

I changed the way business is done in America and throughout the world, and I even have cool hair now. What is left for me? More theories? Yawn. Can't you people come up with one or two of your own? I'm bored. Boredom is another unforeseen result of being smarter than everyone else and rolling in the money I have earned as a result. I wish Einstein were still alive so I could have someone to talk to, but, alas, he is dead.

Time once called me "omniscient, many-armed Hindu god of anecdotes"—where do you go from there?

Anyhow, be careful when aiming for the top. And I'll see you if you get here.

— *Malcolm Gladwell,** published author*

(*As approximated to Gawker by someone who's never met Malcolm Gladwell.)

THE AUTHOR-WRITTEN AMAZON REVIEW

Never write your own reviews on Amazon. What seems like a great idea in your den at 2:00 in the morning will prove to be a regrettable error in judgment. Self-written reviews are more transparent than you think and easily identified by the following markings:

First-person slipups:

☆☆☆☆☆ Intriguing

When I wrote that part about the mystical jellyfish, what the author was getting at was . . .

Praise is paraphrase of press release:

☆☆☆☆☆ Triumphant

This book *really* is a triumph. Author Dan Dannesbury *really does* seem to be both spirited and fierce—the rare original mind set down on paper . . .

Undue emphasis on purchase of book:

☆☆☆☆☆ Essential

At first I borrowed a copy from a friend, but quickly realized I NEEDED TO BUY my own copy! You can't beat book ownership. So, I ran out to BUY, BUY, BUY this excellent book, which seems to be AT EVERY QUALITY BOOKSTORE, IN EVERY CITY. NOW!

Fixation on negative review:

☆☆☆☆☆ **For intelligent readers only**

LitMamaTennessee, you idiot! How can you say such horrible things? Mama, are you sure you even read the book? Mama, what are you talking about 'chapters seem arbitrarily placed, in the midst of action'? Don't you think maybe the author had a reason in mind, a style, Mama? Did that ever even occur to you, or are you too busy being a keyboard-happy breeder? In conclusion, Lit Mother, you shame literature.

Avoid this pitfall by writing a good book that people enjoy.

THINK OUTSIDE THE BOX

THEME: WINE

Most book parties, like art openings, are inherently wine-themed. Wine is the unspoken honoree, the pulsing undercurrent in the room as stacks of brand-new books sit patiently awaiting purchase and signature. Things will not be so confusingly subtle at your wine-themed book party, at which wine is front and center. Why not accentuate this classic book party selling point? A series of 12-foot inflatable wine bottle helium balloons set the tone when guests arrive, instantly dwarfed by their imposing scale. The room is lined on all sides with tables crowded with wine bottles and wine is also rigged to pour from the ceiling (pulley system).

AUTHOR PHOTOS THROUGHOUT TIME

ACKNOWLEDGE IS POWER

The acknowledgments section: ripe with opportunity and yet loaded with career-destroying mines. Here's how to traverse it safely:

Who	The Reality	What to Write
Editor	Made two changes to the entire manuscript.	"Gave me the freedom to find my own voice."
Publisher	Never met.	"Her vision for this book has been invaluable."
Agent	Douche bag who never returns your calls.	"My protector, my bodyguard, my life-line."
Friends	Can't understand why it takes *so long* to publish one book.	"Support has been endless . . ."
Family	Still sending you law school brochures.	"Always encouraged me to pursue my dreams."
Oprah	You watch her show every afternoon.	"This novel is as much hers as mine."
Authors who inspired you	You'd kill your own dog for an endorsement.	"The most brilliant, world-changing writers of our era."
People who said you could never write the book	Motherfuckers.	Thank everyone *in the world* but them, making their omission all the more glaring. (Countless chick-lit authors have clearly adopted this approach.)

From the Desk of...

Jack Sarra

Any logical assumptions you might make about the publishing process are wildly off the mark. As an author you cannot trust your senses, intellect, or intuition. This is because the world of publishing has its own special "fun-house" logic. If you are not already familiar, here's a representative sampling of how things work:

When your publisher presents you with a "Christmastime release date," only after a closer look will you realize that "Christmastime" means December 26. This is especially fun, as you can now look forward to spending the twelve to eighteen months leading up to your release date in a state of cold dread, fearing for the next time someone asks you when your book is coming out.

When you're presented with what you think is a really great book cover "for your approval," and you give your okay, and they say, "Okay, we're running with it," and you say, "Great, I'm so glad my book cover has been finalized and I am very happy with it," that means it's been handed over to a marketing team of thirty so that they can figure out what to change to make the cover suck a bit. Once they're done, you will be presented with an entirely different cover "for your review." Your approval is unnecessary, since the cover is already being printed.

If you ask about a publicity plan for your book, the team will offer DIY suggestions like "Have you heard of MySpace?" and "Do you do graffiti?" and "If you get arrested for anything scandalous, don't cover up your face when you do the perp walk."

If you start to feel cheap, desperate, helpless, or just all around unnecessary, your head is in the right place.

—Jack Sarra, published author

BOOK TO FILM

Congratulations on your best-selling book! Once you've recouped the advance from your publisher, you should have just enough money left over to lease that Ford Probe you've had your eye on. You'll need the car, too, because you'll be responsible for making travel arrangements on your upcoming book tour.

Books are not an especially lucrative medium, as most published authors will tell you. (Particularly if you are their angry landlord or an estranged relative looking for a handout.) To have a truly successful book, it must adapt easily into a successful film. Take, for example, the Harry Potter series, or the novel that inspired Mel Gibson's *The Passion of the Christ*.

Books and film can often seem like two different languages, but the translation is easier than you'd imagine. Follow the rules and examples at right, and you may just parlay your dusty old Booker Prize into a shiny new MTV Movie Award.

THINK OUTSIDE THE BOX

Tip: Guess what? If you "do your best writing" in the shower—all toiletries are a tax write-off. Call your accountant again and tell him L'Occitane sent you!

TITLE

A long or difficult to pronounce (i.e., French) title is fine for the shelves of Barnes & Noble, where customers can sound out the syllables in their heads without fear of embarrassment. However, in line at a multiplex cinema—where you're competing with films like *Crank* and *Speed* and *Explode!*—simplicity is paramount. You don't want to make your audience feel illiterate, especially the ones who *are* illiterate.

Here are some examples of book titles that, with just a bit of tune-up, practically jump off a cinema marquee . . . and into your wallet!

On the Page	On-screen
The Curious Incident of the Dog in the Night-Time, by Mark Haddon	*Doggie Detective*
Everyman, by Philip Roth	**Adam Sandler is** *Everyman*
The Foreign Correspondent: A Novel, by Alan Furst	*Bonjour, Love!*
The Master and Margarita, by Mikhail Bulgakov	*Margaritaville*
The Shell Seekers, by Rosamunde Pilcher	*Just My Luck*
Fraud: The Strategy Behind the Bush Lies and Why the Media Didn't Tell You, by Paul Waldman	*Let Freedom Ring*
Salt: A World History, by Mark Kurlansky	*Tyler Perry's Don't Make Me Take Off My Good Church Shoe and Stomp Your Black Ass, Fool!*

CHARACTERS AND STORY

Hollywood loves a good story. Maybe it's about an underdog rising up to win the Little League World Series, or an underdog rising up to win a date to the prom with a porn star, or the Spanish Civil War. It doesn't matter. As long as it can be explained in less than four seconds, Hollywood will get behind your art.

As for the "stars" of your story, when writing characters, consider this question: "How does this character resemble an actor who can open a tent-pole blockbuster and guarantee at least $100 million in foreign grosses?"

The best way to view your book's characters and their respective narrative journeys is to see them through a Hollywood executive's eyes. Below are some examples of how a film producer might refine your book's heady characters and story to adapt them for cinema success.

On the Page	On-screen
(from *The Whole World Over: A Novel*, by Julia Glass) Greenie Duquette lives a cozy life as a pastry chief in New York's West Village, but has grown tired of her marriage to Alan, a rarely employed psychotherapist whose idealism and passion have long since coalesced into bitterness and self-absorption.	Greenie Chance is about to take a chance . . . on LOVE. Stunningly beautiful but dateless, Greenie is married to her job as a pastry chef. But when the dashing president of the United States tastes one of Greenie's legendary cupcakes and decides to make Greenie his personal live-in chef, it turns out he might have fallen in love with more than her batter. Coming this fall . . . Kate Hudson and George Clooney in *Take the Cake*.

On the Page	On-screen
(From *The Echo Maker,* by Richard Powers) After twenty-seven-year-old truck driver Mark Schluter awakes from a coma with a rare disorder that disconnects visual identifications with emotional ones, his grief-stricken sister enlists the help of a neurologist-turned-bestselling author who is experiencing an identity crisis of his own.	After receiving a head injury in a nitro-cycle accident during a botched covert mission, handsome double-agent Hunter Magnum awakes from a coma thinking he's a suburban FedEx shipping clerk and loving husband. It's up to his sexy spying sidekick, Ava, to help Hunter regain his memory and find out who set him up. Let's just hope they don't fall in love first!! Matthew Fox and Jessica Biel star in. . . Clerk and Dagger!
(from *We Are All Welcome Here,* by Elizabeth Berg) Paige Dunn, stricken by polio at twenty-two during her pregnancy, gives birth to and raises her daughter alone, from the confines of an iron lung, where she is able to move only her head.	The twenty-something Paige Whitmore (Kirsten Dunst), whose sharp tongue is matched only by her incredible looks, is raising her daughter, Lulu, alone in a tiny, cramped Manhattan studio apartment. When Paige (literally!) bumps into Tripp Highway (Matthew McConaughey) at a single-parents' group, she wonders if there's room for two more . . . in her heart. Find out in *Welcome to Love,* coming this spring!

On the Page	On-screen
(from *The Moviegoer,* by Walker Percy) Binx Bolling, a rootless, rakish young man searching for meaning between solitary visits to the cinema.	Binx Blippo is a funny robot with the voice of Dax Shepard, who wants nothing more than to make it as a big movie star. So he packs his fuel tanks, leaves Bolt Junction behind, and heads for the bright, fiber-optic lights of Circuit City (big sponsorship!!).
(from *The Old Man and the Sea,* by Ernest Hemingway) Santiago is an aged Cuban fisherman silently contemplating the capture of a beautiful marlin.	Tom Hanks is a middle-aged architect unsatisfied with his humdrum life. So, on a lazy fishing trip, he gets his sights set on reeling in "Spike," the gigantic swordfish who, legend tells, can grant three wishes if captured. Co-starring Robin Williams as the voice of Spike. *Fishes & Wishes,* coming this summer!!

YOU READ THIS SOMEWHERE

Spearheading the formation of a book club is a great way to catch up with the most annoying people in your neighborhood.

WRITING

Here's how your writing will translate from book to blockbuster.

On the Page	On-screen
Professor Densmore glanced back from his carriage, across the brackish waters, past the tangles of wisteria. There on the furthest banks of Lake Sorrow, his eyes fixed on the old summer house. The carriage lurched forward, and the house grew smaller and smaller—a marble, a speck—then disappeared from sight. "Good riddance, my love," whispered Densmore, then turned forward, never looking back again.	EXT. HIGHWAY—DAY **CORNBREAD,** NO LONGER A VIRGIN, SPEEDS AWAY FROM THE SIGMA PHI HOUSE IN HIS **BRAND-NEW PONTIAC SOLSTICE CONVERTIBLE.** HE CRANKS UP THE STEREO [SONY RECORDING ARTIST TK] AND PUMPS HIS FIST IN TIME WITH THE AWESOME TUNES. CORNBREAD SEES TWO HOT CHICKS HITCHHIKING BY THE SIDE OF THE ROAD. HE SLAMS ON HIS BRAKES AND THE HOT CHICKS SQUEEZE INTO THE PASSENGER SEAT, WHERE THEY BEGIN KISSING EACH OTHER AND RUNNING THEIR FINGERS THROUGH CORNBREAD'S HAIR. CORNBREAD TURNS TO THE CAMERA, LOWERS HIS SUNGLASSES, AND WINKS. cornbread "Onward *Hoze*!" THE PONTIAC PEELS OUT AND SPEEDS OFF AS SMASHMOUTH'S "ALL STAR" BLASTS OVER CLOSING CREDITS.

OPRAH'S BOOK CLUB STICKERS

Designing a sticker for your insanely influential book club? Learn from Oprah's mistakes.

Her current sticker is simple and straightforward:

- Overall Simplicity

- Just 3 Words: Oprah's Book Club

- Bold

- Soothing

But Winfrey's design team traveled a long and winding road to get there, with several hundred wrong turns along the way. Here, in all their misguided glory, are Oprah's Book Club stickers that ultimately did not make the cut.

REJECTED OPRAH'S BOOK CLUB STICKERS

Reason rejected: Gives away the magic formula.

Reason rejected: Seems braggy.

Reason rejected: Symbolism might confuse the sheep who would purchase an Oprah's Book Club book.

Reason rejected: While it is very "sticker-y," ultimately it doesn't say anything about Oprah or the selected book.

Reason rejected: See: "Clip Art Clause" in Oprah's Book Club Sticker Rider.

Reason rejected: The designer is a white guy from South Dakota who doesn't totally understand Oprah's brand.

FIGHT CLUB

If there's anything writers enjoy more than avoiding writing, it's engaging in literary pugilism. It's like real fighting, except the contenders are needle-necked wimps hiding behind colorful word selection. Here's our take on some recent literary battles.

The Players	The Feud	The Winner
Experimental wunderkind Ben Marcus vs. gangly *Corrections* scribe Jonathan Franzen	In an interminable essay in *Harper's*, titled "Why Experimental Fiction Threatens to Destroy Publishing, Jonathan Franzen, and Life as We Know It," Marcus jabs Franzen for abandoning his roots in the avant-grade. While the essay briefly fascinates bloggers—a *Slate* essay by author Jess Row dubs it a lame attempt to "reenact the great prizefights of the past"—Franzen stays in his corner and doesn't respond.	Franzen wins by keeping his mouth shut—for once.
Mauling mandarin Norman Mailer vs. sharp-hitting *New York Times* critic Michiko Kakutani	In an interview in *Rolling Stone*, Mailer lashes out at Kakutani—who compared his memoir, *The Spooky Art,* to "going on a very long bus ride over a very bumpy road, sitting next to a garrulous raconteur who never takes a nap and never pauses for breath"—dubbing the critic a "kamikaze" and a "twofer," a token employee of the *Times*. Kakutani remains mum, but a public discussion between Mailer and the Asian American Journalists Association ensues.	Kakutani wins. Kakutani *always* wins.

The Players	The Feud	The Winner
Youthful sensation Colson Whitehead vs. middle-aged warhorse Richard Ford	Reviewing Ford's 2002 story collection, *A Multitude of Sins*, Whitehead complains that "the characters are nearly indistinguishable. If I were an epidemiologist, I'd say that some sort of spiritual epidemic had overtaken a segment of our nation's white middle-class professionals and has started to afflict white upper-middle-class professionals." Snap! Two years later, Ford approaches Whitehead at a literary party and says, "I've waited two years for this! You spat on my book." Ford then spits on him.	Ford's Naomi Campbell–caliber meltdown results in a loss.
Pointy-headed critic William Logan vs. two-fisted Pulitzer Prize winner Franz Wright	Writing in *The New Criterion*, Logan calls Wright's poem "rancid and repetitive" and the poet himself a "sad-sack punk." In a letter to the editor, Wright promises to give Logan "the crippling beating you so clearly masochistically desire."	*The New Criterion?* Everyone loses.
Lethal lightweight Dale Peck vs. seasoned rage-aholic Stanley Crouch	In a 2000 review of Crouch's novel *Don't the Moon Look Lonesome*, Peck calls the book "a terrible novel, badly conceived, badly executed, and put forward in bad faith; reviewing it is like shooting fish in a barrel." Asked about the reviewer in 2002, Crouch calls Peck "a troubled queen." Then, on a summer afternoon in 2004, Crouch slaps Peck in the face at Manhattan eatery Tartine.	Peck haters score a vicarious thrill, but Crouch is disqualified.

The Players	The Feud	The Winner
Gangly *Corrections* scribe Jonathan Franzen vs. cross-media heavyweight Oprah Winfrey	After *The Corrections* is selected for Oprah's Book Club, Franzen expresses misgivings about having an Oprah sticker slapped on the cover and about being selected at all. "I like to read entertaining books and this maybe helps bridge that gap, but it also heightens these feelings of being misunderstood," he says. Winfrey disinvites him and moves on to the next book.	Everyone loses when Oprah stops selecting fiction for her Book Club— unless, of course, it's marketed as nonfiction.
Feisty veterans Tom Wolfe, Norman Mailer, John Irving and John Updike	After Updike and serial brawler Mailer turn poisonous pens on Wolfe's 1998 novel *A Man in Full*—Updike calls it "entertainment, not literature," while Mailer compares it to "making love to a three-hundred-pound woman"—Wolfe dismisses them as "two piles of bones." Joining the Battle Royal, Irving defends both piles of bones on Canadian TV and describes Wolfe's fiction as "yak." Wolfe later dubs the trio "the Three Stooges."	Who cares? Old people are funny.

TOP AUTHORS START YOUNG!

1   Addiction, addiction, addiction. Get hooked on heroin, gambling, self-cutting, shopping, or close your eyes, open a dictionary and find a word. Become obsessed with it somehow.

2   Take a three-day trip to Iraq or become a teacher in the ghetto for a week.

3   Be sure your parents abuse or neglect you. If they're not cooperating, try annoying them until they do.

4   If you are normal and likable, put on a wig and sunglasses and say you are depressed and were sold into sex slavery by insane relative.

IMPORTANT: Pick a relative who is going to die soon or who has Alzheimer's disease, so that they will be unable to disagree with narrative.

POWER SENTENCE: "When I was humbly working on this book, alone, by a low-wattage bulb, I had NO idea it would become such a cultural milestone."

Literary Star To-Do List

✓ Write Novel.

✓ On title page, highlight words "a novel," delete, and write "a memoir."

✓ Send out to agents. Work with the agent who wears the most expensive shoes.

✓ Have agent set up an interview on Oprah. Go on Oprah. IMPORTANT: DO NOT GET HER ANGRY.

3 PRINT

MANY OF YOU THINK of the *New York Times* as an online publication. Did you know it had its origins in the world of print? Print = newspapers, magazines, journals, and such. Writing on paper. It still exists.

NEWS TO YOU?

"TK" is an abbreviation journalists can use in an early draft of their writing to indicate they're going to fill in a particular detail later, after conducting further research. So, a first stab at a music article might include a sentence that reads: "*TK white kids bought 50 Cent albums last year, whereas TK white adults did.*" Or a draft of a field report might read: "*TK journalists were killed in Afghanistan and Pakistan, including Geraldo Rivera . . .*" Once the research is complete, a real number is substituted in and the TK removed.

This is a great little system, but be aware that it can present last-minute problems for procrastinators. As it turns out, excessive reliance on the TK can result in a lackluster writing style (approximated below):

> "*TK TK TK TK TK TK TK TK TK TK TK TK TK TK. TK TK TK TK TK TK TK TK! TK TK TK TK TK TK TK TK TK TK TK TK TK TK TK! TK TK TK TK TK TK TK TK TK TK TK TK, TK TK TK TK. TK TK TK TK TK TK TK TK TK TK; TK TK TK TK TK TK TK TK TK TK TK TK TK TK . . . TK TK . . .*"

To illustrate usage, we've left a few wild "TKs" here or there throughout this book. If you catch one, pat yourself on the back. That's extra credit, eagle eyes.

THE MASTHEAD

A given publication's "masthead" reflects the official pecking order of all staff. A masthead is also called a "banner" or "nameplate" by people who are more eccentric than they need to be. Mastheads should have your rapt attention. Scour them regularly for new names and scandalous trades.

There are many ways to organize a masthead, all of them illustrating a rank and file, hierarchical workplace, in which almost everyone is below someone else.

Here are a few mastheads, with different organizing principles at play.

Standard Masthead

Editor in Chief

Executive Editor

Deputy Editor

Creative Director

Managing Editor

Articles Editor

Senior Editor

Editor at Large

Assistant Managing Editor

Associate Editor

Assistant Editor

Editorial Assistant

Chief Assistant

Assistancier

Assistant Assistancier

Tits 'n' Associate

Associate Editor's Girlfriend's Dog

Intern

Starbucksian Masthead

Applied to editorial positions, this could make the workweek a lot less confusing. You'd instantly understand whose ass to kiss to get a promotion (Venti Editor) and who to send for cigarettes and then never reimburse them because they'll feel too nervous to bring it up (Tall Editor).

☐ **Venti Editor**
☐ **Grande Editor**
☐ **Tall Editor**

Masthead with X-ray Glasses

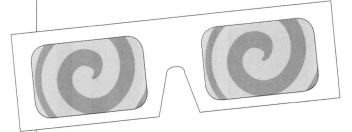

Ed in Chief
Glorified Intern 1
Glorified Intern 2
Glorified Intern 3
Glorified Intern 4
Glorified Intern 5

WHO'S MORE POWERFUL—
ASSISTANT EDITOR OR *EDITORIAL ASSISTANT*?

The answer is that most people would have no idea because the two titles sound identical to the naked ear. Most people would be annoyed by the very question and how it was interrupting their favorite episode of *I Love New York*. Let's be clear. No matter how you slice the pie, each slice is basically equivalent to $30 thou a year, plus or minus taxes and varying perks. Still, Associate and Assistant sound too close.

Job titles in publishing could be simple and straightforward—just like other job titles, e.g., "Carpenter" or "Warlord." Someone shows up for their first day at work as a carpenter and they know what is expected of them, they know they're gonna build some shit. Warlords strategize how to blow things up and make people die. You say: "Warlord, meet guerrilla fighter" and the two have an immediate sense of each other's strengths, and of their working relationship.

THE GAWKER GUIDE TO CONQUERING ALL MEDIA

WHICH MAG SHOULD YOU BE RUNNING?

Work at a magazine that best reflects your personality, and your leap to Editor-in-Chief status is all but assured. Scan the magazine titles listed in bold and ask yourself the questions listed below each one. If you answer yes to at least one, you've pinpointed the masthead your name should crown.

Do you pretend to be ironic about things you actually like?

Do you feel "more safer" reading when reading feels like watching TV?

Do you take breaks from watching TV on TV in order to watch TV on the internet?

People

Do you actually care for celebrities, like you cry when something bad happens to them?

AMERICAN THEATRE

Are you boring and gay, counter to the positive stereotype of "interestingness" and gayness being closely related?

Do you use words like "indeed" in your casual conversations?

Stuff /MAXIM

Are you so straight you're borderline gay?

Do you describe yourself as a "tit guy" in your twenty online dating profiles?

Do you feel you're nothing without your cars and watches?

Do you feel like a homo without a big-boobed companion beside you at events?

Do you feel like a homo with a big-boobed companion beside you at events?

Come on, are you a homo or what?

WALL STREET JOURNAL

Do you "love" prostitutes and "really enjoy" your wife?

Do you know what it's like to screw a twelve-year-old (figuratively or literally), due to your many business-related travels?

"Steak avec Drugs et Whores." Sound like the high-end restaurant of your dreams?

ESSENCE

Do you have expensive ethnic art in your brownstone?

Are you trying to build a career sensibly?

Purchase a home sensibly?

Find a man sensibly?

Eat sensibly?

Sleep sensibly?

Do you often give praise?

Do you crave advice from experts and PhDs?

Are you sensual, proud, spiritual, intelligent, and confident? Yes you ARE!

O

Are you one part crazy?

Are you nine parts housewife?

When it comes to literature, film, or music, do you love to cry for hours?

If it existed, would "poignant" be your favorite genre?

Is your life fueled by the observation of other people's personal revelations?

VIBE

Were you cool a decade ago?

Do you like swearing but find it doesn't come natural?

When it comes to magazine writing, do you abhor the "angle"?

Do you savor simple profiles on celebs and model citizens?

Do you tend to rise to the challenge of reading itsy-bitsy fonts?

JET

Do you like to receive issues fifty-two times a year?

RADAR

Do you enjoy regular periods of unemployment/constant uncertainty?

Is "failure" an option you're forced to take three to four times a year?

If at first you don't succeed, do you try and try and try and try and try and try again?

NATIONAL GEOGRAPHIC

Do you often find yourself using the word "nubile"?

Are you intimidated and mystified by the complicated ways of your own people (i.e., the Americans, the Europeans)?

ELLE

What's your absolute bottom line for scented candles? Is it $35/candle?

VOGUE

Would you describe your personality as cold or very cold?

Does spending $2,000 on mink eyelash extensions strike you as a need?

W

Are you sort of running out of ways to blow through your money because it keeps continuing to earn interest on itself?

Is your dog small, very small, or incredibly small?

BoatingLife

Has your relationship to cocaine become unmanageable?

Did your father make you feel sooo small?

Good Housekeeping

Are you terrified of divorce?

Has your relationship to Purell become unmanageable?

Rolling Stone

Are you balding yet "with ponytail"?

Are you wearing a leather vest right now and almost always?

Entertainment Weekly

Are you sort of blah?

Vice

Do you think shit, cum, cocaine, and hot girls are all equally interesting?

The Nation

Do you feel exploited by the very things that make other people happy (movies, sex, TV, clothing, cologne, mac 'n' cheese)?

Do you hate magazines yet yearn to read them?

ADBUSTERS

Is "Society" totally on your shit list?

Do you only buy vintage Nike?

PENTHOUSE

Are you a romantic who still believes in love?

Do you simply refuse to settle for anything less than story-book encounters?

Parents

Was your pregnancy planned to the day?

VANITY FAIR

Do you pepper your speech with British expressions, despite having grown up in Wichita?

Do you regret being a bit too old to qualify as an enfant terrible?

Are you the type of successful yet boring guy who takes three women out on the exact same date each week?

PAPER

Do you have this book in one hand and a mirror in the other?

Are you a freelance stylist?

Do you get really passionate about arugula and break dancing?

WORD UP

Do you prefer one-syllable words to multisyllabic?

Do you think of sixteen-year-old boys as "hot babes" or "sexy dudes"?

Do you like dismantling a magazine in order to enjoy the fruits of your labor, which are 18,000 posters of Chris Brown?

Do you take Ne-Yo seriously as performer and man?

If you could dance like anyone in the world . . . would it totally be Ciara?!?!!

THINK OUTSIDE THE BOX

Tip: Looking to make a few extra bucks? Why not sublet your boss's office on Craig's List to a freelancer who works nights? Or eBay an office chair. No one will notice and they can go for upwards of $900. No matter what chair you have, here are some details to include in your description: pneumatic lift seat height adjustment, tilt tension, ergonomic design, graphite frame, adjustable arms (flip up), knee rest attachment, leather upholstery, 360-degree swivel—fully assembled.

TRUE TALENT

What is seen as talent in publishing falls into three categories. As soon as you identify which category you fall into, you'll be better able to sell yourself. How do you market "You"?

TIMELINESS ("THE DEADLINER")

Hardworking, meets all deadlines (even gets things in before deadlines), meets page count requirement to the letter.

Your burning question: Am I better at putting words onto the page than making them sound good?

How to angle yourself: "I can get that to you two days after you assign it. Remarkable, isn't it? Don't read it."

EGO ("THE ME GUY")

Mouthy, smug, rude, proud, ballsy, renegade, risk taker . . .

Your burning question: If I take a quiet moment of honest introspection, do I arrive at the conclusion that I'm the best writer to have ever lived?

How to angle yourself: "You could always go to someone else for something uninspired and derivative. Or I could breathe life into your flailing little operation and put you guys back on the map."

TALENT ("PUDDING")

The proof is in the pudding with this one.

Your burning question: I'm bored, and have some excellent writing to do. May I be excused from this career guide?

How to angle yourself: "Here are some clips. Here's a great idea. Let me know if you will pay me the amount I require."

CLIPS: WHAT DOESN'T COUNT AS A WRITING SAMPLE

- High school philosophy paper

- Senior thesis

- Entire PhD dissertation

- Exquisitely penned "roommate wanted" ad

- A lengthy Mother's Day card

- Your cover letter

- Completed crossword puzzle

MEET YOUR NEW BEST FRIEND:
THE CORPORATE CARD

If you work at a magazine and you're not an idiot, you'll figure out how to expense everything from a pack of gum to your last colonoscopy. Some examples:

Cabs

The rule: Everything—dinner with friends, trips to museums or the theater, even shopping—can be considered work. Hence, every cab you ever take can be considered a work-related expense. Even a cab used for a 5 A.M. drug run.

Drinks

The rule: If your buddy works in *any* capacity that is vaguely connected to media—PR is ideal or just someone who really likes reading magazines— then your friendship can be heavily subsidized, if not fully expensed.

Grooming

The rule: if you need to look a certain part at a major work event, chances are you can get reimbursed for the styling efforts required. Don't push your luck with Sally Hershberger's tab if you're in the middle of the masthead— but, within reason, looking good can go on the company bill. (Your last five microdermabrasions were within reason.)

Keep Up

The rule: Anything that enhances your general understanding of the general world your magazine covers should be considered an expense. If you work at *O: The Oprah Magazine*, you're not paying for Deepak's latest. If you work at *Maxim*, you're not paying for Jenna Jameson's latest. It's called "keep up," it's delightfully vague, and it's every magazine employee's best friend.

THE PITCH NO ONE CAN SAY NO TO

Editors are fickle, and pitching is a fragile courtship. Writer and editor exchange careful emails that often amount to nothing beyond hand-holding and literary blue balls. If you want that holy grail pub to stop being coy and take you in at long last, you gotta Don Juan it. You gotta Mike Tyson it, until "no" is simply not an option.

When it comes to a pitch email, all that matters is how you get in and how you get out. Don't start with "You seem so powerful . . ." Don't be too familiar ("Dude, thought you'd love this shit, haha, I wrote it on mescaline . . ."), or too jokey ("The attached manuscript is in invisible ink . . . JUST KIDDING! Oh, man! I'm cracking myself up, so I KNOW you gotta be smilin'!").

Here's the formula you need:

Powerful greeting

+

Short description of your idea

+

Gentle exit

=

SOLID PITCH LETTER!

YOU READ THIS SOMEWHERE

In her forties, Jessica Alba will be featured in a magazine erroneously reporting: "These are the best years of my life."

SAMPLE IRRESISTIBLE PITCH LETTERS

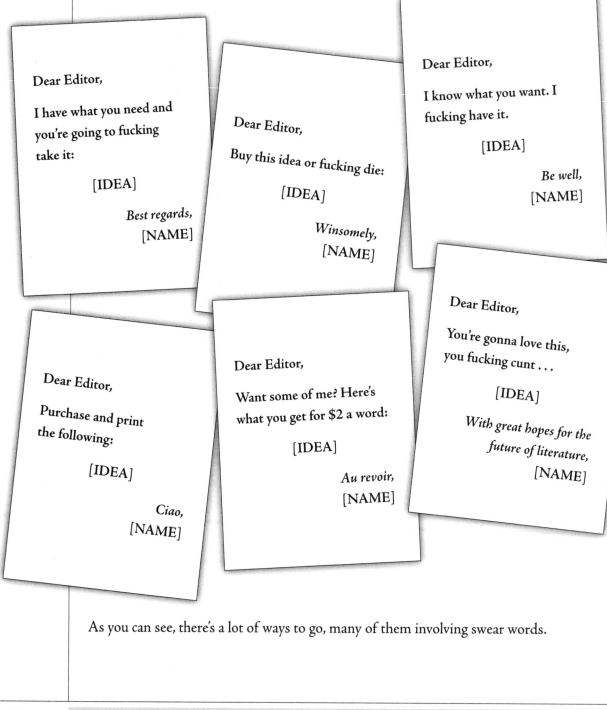

Dear Editor,

I have what you need and you're going to fucking take it:

[IDEA]

Best regards,
[NAME]

Dear Editor,

Buy this idea or fucking die:

[IDEA]

Winsomely,
[NAME]

Dear Editor,

I know what you want. I fucking have it.

[IDEA]

Be well,
[NAME]

Dear Editor,

Purchase and print the following:

[IDEA]

Ciao,
[NAME]

Dear Editor,

Want some of me? Here's what you get for $2 a word:

[IDEA]

Au revoir,
[NAME]

Dear Editor,

You're gonna love this, you fucking cunt . . .

[IDEA]

With great hopes for the future of literature,
[NAME]

As you can see, there's a lot of ways to go, many of them involving swear words.

STORY IDEAS NO WOMEN'S MAGAZINE CAN RESIST

Fill in the blanks for a $2 a word beauty mag pitch.

Lose ____ pounds in ____ days just by ____!

Deflab your ____!

New beauty products that will ____ your ____!

Hot off the runways: _____ that shine!

____ must-haves, straight from ____!

Feeling _____? Feel _____ in three easy steps!

____ for every age!

You ___ piece of ___. You disgust everyone. Try ____ or ____ or give up entirely. You're a real sack of ____, you know that? Does your ____ look like it's stuffed with Grape Nuts? Then do ___, ____, and ____, sh_thead.

YOU READ THIS SOMEWHERE

In 2006, Saddam Hussein owned a 2 percent stake in Lagardère, the French parent company of Hachette Filipacchi. This explains why 2 percent of articles in Elle Girl *were about beatings, rape, and shock torture.*

SUB STANDARDS

Readerships, rate bases, newsstand and subscription sales: with so many terms, it can be hard to decode just how large (or small) a magazine's circulation is. Here's a quick equivalency guide—with real-world examples—for a few well-known titles.

30,000,000 •

Circulation of biodegradable ad trap *Parade*—the most widely distributed magazine in the United States, which appears as an extraneous blow-in in more than three hundred Sunday newspapers.

Number of Americans with "below basic" literacy skills.

3,000,000 •

Circulation of oversexed glossy *Cosmopolitan*.

Annual number of new chlamydia infections nationwide.

3,000,000 •

Circulation of faith-based magazine *Guideposts*, "America's Source of Hope and Inspiration."

George Bush's margin of victory in the 2004 presidential election.

2,100,000 •

Circulation of glossy gateway drug *Seventeen*.

Number of cosmetic surgeries performed in 2006.

1,300,000 ▪

Circulation of glossy gateway drug *CosmoGirl!*

Number of cosmetic procedures performed on teenagers since 2000.

715,000 ▪

Circulation of *Harper's Bazaar.*

Circulation of *Harper's*—multiplied by π.

35,000 ▪

Circulation of *Variety,* the daily bible of the entertainment industry.

Number of people in Los Angeles County who have experienced four episodes of homelessness in the last three years—not including Natasha Lyonne.

14 ▪

Circulation of *Park Slope Reader.*

Number of days in two weeks.

ALL THE DIRT THAT'S FIT TO PRINT

The gossip pages can play a vital role in your personal PR efforts. Whether you're trying to get a tidbit into the columns or keep your name out of them, it's important to know whom you're dealing with and how to work them to your advantage. Our handy diagram (next page) outlines how to get the best out of the major gossip players in New York City.

	Cindy Adams	Liz Smith	Jeannette Walls
Publication	*NY Post*, "Cindy Adams"	*NY Post*, "Liz Smith"	MSNBC.com (via *New York* magazine)
Known For	Addressing old people (her readers) as "kids."	Celeb rim jobs, in print.	Went from eating trash to writing it.
Celebs He/She Loves to Buzz About	International royalty, Upper East Side royalty, and old Hollywood starlets.	Fab dead people + the nearly dead: Ivana, Liza, Camilla.	Anorexics. If you don't eat dinner, she's on it!
How to Get in His/Her Good Graces	Drown yourself in her perfume, Gossip. If you use enough, it'll penetrate the two holes in her face that represent a nose.	Throw this Texas gal a down-home BBQ.	Leave a nice meal in the garbage for her mom.
The Best Way to Piss Him/Her Off	Stomp her Yorkie Jazzy to death to the tune of "All That Jazz."	Call her Cindy Adams.	Repeatedly refer to her fucked-up family in your chart about NYC gossip columnists.
Celeb They Most Resemble	If Lucille Ball fucked a Komodo dragon in an Estée Lauder factory.	Ted Koppel.	East Hampton Jane Seymour.
Buddhist Tenet They Most Embody	To overcome Suffering, it is necessary to escape the Cycle of life and death; to escape the Cycle of life and death, it is necessary to extinguish Desire; and to extinguish Desire, it is necessary to destroy Ignorance.	The dispersion of Ignorance can be attained by the persevering practice of an all-embracing Altruism of Conduct, development of Wisdom, and Non-attachment for the transitory objects of ego-grasping.	There is no independent absolute "I."

Ben Widdicombe	Rush & Molloy	Paula Froelich	Richard Johnson
New York Daily News, "Ben Widdicombe's Gatecrasher"	*New York Daily News*, "Rush & Molloy"	*NY Post* "Page Six"	*NY Post* "Page Six"
Gayness, blind items. Hot for a gossip columnist.	Being married. Vow to love and honor each other in sickness, health, and celebrity obsession.	Challenging Tara Reid to a Jell-O wrestling match.	King of the greatest gossip column in the universe.
Studio execs and other Hollywood hotties caught pants down with members of the same sex.	*Today* show anchors and the models and moguls who love them.	Whoever Lizzie Grubman tells her to buzz about— Botoxed blonds of a feather stick together.	Anybody who can't pay for privacy.
Compliment his looks— in an Australian way!	Schmooze with the assistants who do all their work.	Tell her you read her book (*It!: 9 Secrets of the Rich and Famous That'll Take You to the Top*) and that it was more inspiring than any other gossip wag–penned guide to success you've ever read.	$.
Tell him Hayden Christensen is straight.	Refer to column by their assistants' last names.	Tell her that you only got to page 6 of her book.	"Dude, how come Page Six isn't on page 6?"
A tan, blond Christian Slater.	A poor man's Cybill Shepherd and Bruce Willis, circa the *Moonlighting* years.	Cate Blanchett.	Imagine Peter Gallagher, now minus the brows . . . even creepier.
The seeker of Truth can transcend created existence and attain, through spiritual practice and mystical contemplation, a supreme state of peace called Nirvana.	No one should believe what is spoken by any sage, written in any scripture, or affirmed by any tradition unless it accords with reason.	To refrain from all sin. To practice virtue. To purify the Heart.	The Universe functions according to a natural law of causation known as "Karma." The wholesome and unwholesome actions of a being in past existences determine his condition in the present life. Each man, therefore, has prepared the causes of the effects which he now experiences.

NEW YORK POST HEADLINES

In the dog-eat-dog world of print journalism, the reader looks to the snappiest headline. The *New York Post* has cornered the market on the retardedly mesmerizing front page.

Here are four easy tricks to the art of crafting a *Post* headline:

1   *Word play.* Go bananas, you fucking monkey.

2   *Hyphens.* Hy-FUNS!

3   *Replace S with dollar sign ($).* This helps visual learners!

4   **Adapt an adage to vaguely apply to the news story.** People love a new twist on an old cliché.

Now that you know the tricks, try to guess if the following headlines are real headlines (R), or fakes (F):

1   **HAWKS' EGGS-PIRATION DATE**

2   **SNOOZE'S PHOTO "OOPS"**

3   **RANDY DON'S RENDEZ-RUSE**

4   **DIABETIC HEIRESS SWEET ON HANDBAGS**

5   **AXIS OF WEASEL**

6   **LAY YOUR HEAD ON MY BOULDER**

7   **MUCH A-DOO ABOUT SOMETHIN!**

8   **DOG EAT HOG WORLD!**

9   **PAIN IN THE GAS**

10   **HEADLESS BODY IN TOPLESS BAR**

11   **SADDAM, BAM, THANK YOU MA'AM**

1: R; 2: R; 3: R; 4: F; 5: amazingly R; 6: F; 7: F; 8: F; 9: R; 10: R; 11: F.

INTERN AS MEASURE OF SUCCESS

A developing career can be measured in interns.

1 intern = Up and Comer.

5 interns = Solid Start.

10 = A few powerful people vaguely know of you.

30 = "Good morning, sir."
(Whether you're a guy or a girl.)

100 = "Which charity
would you like to start
today, Mr. Gates?"

300 = One of Oprah's interns

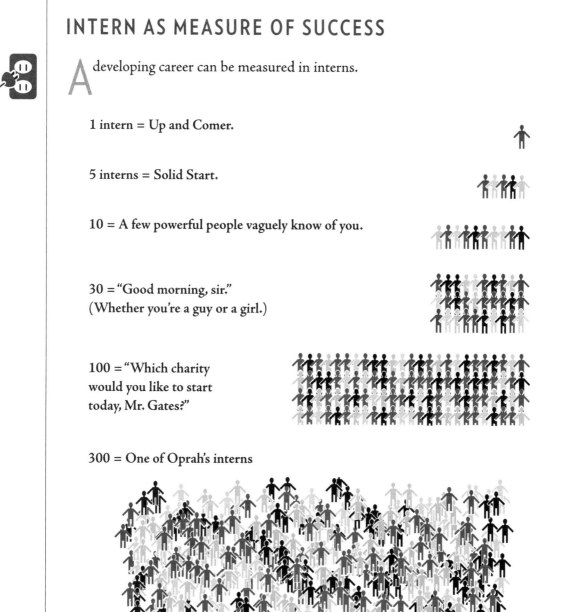

4 RADIO

ARE YOU HORRIBLY DISFIGURED and/or 400 pounds? There's still room for you in the media landscape. Get ready to teach the airwaves a violent lesson.

COMMON SITUATIONS IN MORNING RADIO AND HOW TO HANDLE THEM LIKE A PRO

- *Situation:* You've been asked to record some promotional spots for a summer concert.

  What to Do: Shout it, beginning to end.

- *Situation:* Caller has radio on.

  What to Do: Shout at them to turn it down.

- *Situation:* Caller is caller number X—meaning they've won your call-in.

  What to Do: Shout at them to shout the name of your radio station.

- *Situation:* You've just made a funny joke.

  What to Do: Now shout it again! Shout the punch line repeatedly. This is your moment to shout!

- *Situation:* Producer is hitting wrong buttons.

  What to Do: Complain via mouth-shouting.

- *Situation:* Accidental dead air.

  What to Do: Come back and blame someone in a very loud voice. It's basically a shout you'd be using here.

QUIZ: WHAT KIND OF RADIO PERSONALITY TYPE ARE YOU?

Ever yell at the TV when the local news is on?

   a.   Local news . . . you mean the *MacNeil-Lehrer News Hour?*

   b.   I like it when they do a report on kittens!

   c.   Nope . . . too busy watching German scrunt porn.

When you look in the mirror you see . . .

   a.   An intelligent, sincere human being.

   b.   Lots of dyed blond hair and nothing a nose job won't fix.

   c.   A bloody eye, Ted Kennedy's nose, and a face tattoo.

When you see a plus-sized woman walking down the street you think . . .

   a.   We need a law to eliminate trans fat from all foods nationwide.

   b.   I hope I don't end up looking like that. Better throw up my lunch.

   c.   I want to make her fuck a midget.

You're at a party and someone asks for your opinion on a subject you know nothing about. You . . .

   a.   Pull out your BlackBerry and do some research. How can you make an informed opinion without the facts?

   b.   Flash your tits.

   c.   State your opinion loudly. Facts are for fags.

When you are alone at night, you fantasize about . . .

   a.   Alan Greenspan.

   b.   Pudding!

   c.   Dakota Fanning.

When President Bush gives a speech on prime time television, you . . .

   a.   Take copious notes and send an editorial to *Mother Jones* magazine.

   b.   Wonder if *Fear Factor* is mad at you and hiding from you.

   c.   Agree with everything he says.

You refer to your significant other as . . .

   a.   My life partner.

   b.   Daddy!

   c.   Cunt.

You and your friends decide to go out for some drinks at 7:00 p.m. You have an on-air radio shift at 9:00 a.m. do you . . .

   a.   Order hot water and lemon; it is very soothing to the voice.

   b.   Have one chocolate martini and discuss which *Sex and the City* girl you are.

   c.   Fuck the waitress in the bathroom, buy some meth, and commit a hate crime.

When you see a baseball bat you think . . .

   a.   I love Ken Burns's documentary on the subject.

   b.   Pudding!

   c.   How far inside a woman can I place this without doing permanent damage . . . to my ratings!?!

When you see a person of color, you think . . .

   a.   I'm proud that our nation is so diverse.

   b.   Bill Cosby!

   c.   Al Qaeda.

Your idea of a perfect morning radio show consists of . . .

   a.   Unbiased news, interesting editorials, and maybe a puzzle . . . just for fun.

   b.   The 3 Gs: grooves, gossip and guffaws!

   c.   Fisting a woman while playing fart sound effects.

Your typical Saturday usually consists of . . .

a. Volunteering at the soup kitchen, then bathing the cats.

b. Hip-hop dance class then being refused at Nobu.

c. Community service.

If you answered mostly

a. Hello, Smartie Pants! You need a gig on NPR or Air America. Congratulations, you're about to enter a world of people who also appreciate jazz.

b. Your lack of curiosity about the world makes you a perfect weather and traffic girl on a Top 40 station. Better get implants!

c. I smell a shock jock! What you consider funny breaks the Geneva Convention on torture but fits perfectly into drive-time radio. Congratulations on your syndication deal!

RADIO CALL-IN ADVICE

Get the caller's name, repeat it over and over.

Mock. Act concerned. Mock. Act concerned.

Rant about a topic that you always rant about (free associate).

Hang up the second you're bored.

Remember: Your personality is bigger than the caller's problem.

RADIO STUDIO WALL HANGING

Here is the golden rule of morning radio. Hang it up in your studio so you can refer to it throughout your shift:

WHEN IN DOUBT,
SHOUT!

AUDIO CUES FOR MORNING
RADIO SHOWS: A CHECKLIST

Is my audio cue:

- ☐ Loud enough? (Is it so loud it almost has a smell?)

- ☐ Is it high-pitched enough?

- ☐ Does it last long enough?

- ☐ Would it wake a very deep sleeper on sleeping pills?

- ☐ Is it a sound not commonly heard in the natural world?

HOW TO GENERATE BUZZ IN TALK RADIO

There are at least a dozen radio shows in every major market that feature the same electrifying format of "man/woman offers opinion into microphone. Caller responds." Here's how to stay on top of the heap:

- Ignore your personal politics. They're completely irrelevant. No one who wants "rational" is listening to AM radio at five o'clock in the morning. "This guy's crazy" is a far more desirable effect than "Okay, that makes sense."

- Hang up on at least one caller an hour. Doesn't matter why. After they've gone, call them stupid/moron/loser. This will show listeners that their "A game" is required when calling you, even though you deliver a C+ game, at best.

- Avoid reporting the actual news. Boring! Take it from Gawker: If people wanted real information, they'd be reading newspapers.

- Start a feud with another talk radio host, ideally based on opposing beliefs. Make sure they know about it. If wavering on this policy, ask yourself "Who made more money off the Bill O'Reilly/Al Franken mêlée, us or them?"

YOU READ THIS SOMEWHERE

Radio commercials are designed by sound engineers to make you want to buy products and/or kill yourself.

WHAT CAN WE LEARN FROM THE MASTERS?

Study 'n' Steal:

Imus in the Morning: 1200 hamburgers to go? YES. Nappy-headed hos? NO! (See "Who to Humorlessly Revere in Talk Radio").

The Howard Stern Show: Radio listeners desperate for sexual intimacy can listen to the *sound* of a naked woman and get excited. What does a naked woman sound like? Ratings. If you can find a way to further humiliate the women while naked, such as throwing deli meat at their backsides, national syndication is likely.

The Opie & Anthony Show: If you're hesitant to do crazy things yourself, have listeners do them for you. No decent human being would have sex in a church; however, encouraging listeners to do so is fantastic radio. One note of caution: your program director and local archdiocese may not agree. In this case you'll be fired. Worry not—the press will make you more famous and your next contract will make you very rich. ("Whip 'em out Wednesdays" are cool with everybody, probably even God). Then just avoid having a homeless guy talk about banging the secretary of state during the Imus blowup.

The Tom Joyner Show: Danger is not for everyone. In fact, many listeners like to play it as safe as humanly possible in the morning. Therefore, if your personality is inherently bland, embrace it and program accordingly. Perform comedic bits that your listeners are comfortable with, such as those they have already come to enjoy on other programs. A Top 10 list can be made your own when transformed into a Top 5 list. They'll recognize the structure, but appreciate your creative spin.

The Rush Limbaugh Show: Don't be afraid to pass judgment on benign public figures. Facts aren't important. So what if Donovan McNabb is a Super Bowl quarterback? It's possible he's only famous because he's black. And even though Michael J. Fox has a serious illness, it's conceivable he's embellishing for sympathy. "The" truth is less important than "your" truth. If you find the mental burden of your posturing too great to bear, indulge in prescription pain medication by the handful.

The Wendy Williams Experience: With a smile in your voice, ask celebrities painful personal questions. Cough, talk about snacks you like, talk about your husband and your son, repeat. Drink champagne on air for hours straight while you rue your days as an "ex-offender" cokehead who has mercifully cleaned up. Encourage your listeners to diet and get plastic surgery. Be super into your hair, makeup, body, and attire. Hire a butch male sidekick to straighten the Gays 'n' Gals slant of your following.

Note: *Most liberal radio programs omitted, due to utter lack of success in the field (for liberal achievements in entertainment, see TV AND FILM).*

HOW TO GIVE ADVICE IN THE TRADITION OF WBLS RADIO WAG WENDY WILLIAMS

Three simple sentences will keep listeners calling for your "special take" on their lives time and time again:

1 "You're too young to be in this type of relationship. Break up."

2 "You're too old to be in this type of relationship. Break up."

3 "If you've been together so long, why aren't you married?"

CRUCIAL STAFF MEMBERS
IN TALK RADIO HOSTING

Hosting is a moderately difficult job, and you can't do it on your own. The right support staff assures mega-success with very little work from you.

Board Operator. Has expert timing with a range of crucial sound effects, such as: crickets, record scratching, flatulence (loud), flatulence (soft), flatulence (airy), flatulence (wet), flatulence (wet, then sort of trumpet-like), cat hissing (for female interaction), diva-type voice using ethnic terminology (e.g., "Whatch yoo say?!")

Call Screeners. Accept blame when you misunderstand the caller's name or topic.

Talent Booker. In spite of zero awareness of pop culture and limited interpersonal skills, the booker is always able to usher a warm body of some sort into the studio.

Interns. Are used for production tasks that would normally receive compensation: cleaning of bathrooms, forging autographs, photocopying, drinking vomit, et cetera.

Sidekick. Person in studio who is paid to laugh. Otherwise, listeners won't know you're being funny.

Sexy and/or Sassy Producer. Lends your show credibility, though their true function is to be a soft "on-air personality." No skills needed; only requirement is the genuine desire to build a production résumé.

General Manager or Program Director. "Stuffed-shirt" superior. Cuts you down to size so your listeners will relate to you. Complain about them often, but behind closed doors, cede to these guys' every request. They hold the money.

WHO TO HUMORLESSLY REVERE IN TALK RADIO (ON FEAR OF FIRING)

With the recent rounds of high-profile firings and suspensions in talk radio, one can never be too careful. To keep your seat, adopt an attitude of reverence toward everything imaginable. If you can think of it, chances are you'd better revere it. Otherwise a top representative from some watchdog group will come after you, advertisers will panic, and your talk radio career will be in flames before you can hang up your headphones.

Earnestness and reverence may sound boring, but they . . . are. Anyhow, some tips:

RADIO SCANDAL POINTERS:

DON'T offer an apology if you say something that causes a sudden media blitz. You're going to be fired anyway, and watchdog groups don't "forgive and forget." (That attitude would take them off payroll.)

DO pinpoint a particular voice of minority pride and label *them* as being racist, if your scandal is race related. Consider: Jesse Jackson, Brenda Howard, Gandhi, et al. No one expects it, it relieves you of some heat, and it causes quite a stir. Use the phrase(s) "reverse racism" and/or "hypocrite" and/or "double-standards."

DON'T involve Al Sharpton. Don't meet with him, don't guest on his radio show, don't face off with him on the evening news. His job is to throw fuel on the flames and there's nothing you can do to affect that. If he does come after you, try to adopt a peaceful wait-and-see attitude about whether his crusade will elevate your radio scandal to front-page firing status.

From the Desk of...

Jim Norton

⌇

Shock Jocks. Yuck. It's a term I've really come to hate, and I resent the fact that all male-oriented talk shows have been lumped into this category. As producer of the *Henderson & AIDS Morning Show,* I am constantly barraged with questions about the integrity of our show. The reason we make the money we do is because we provide an entertaining service, which translates into ratings, which translates into advertising revenue. Year in and year out, our annual Pig Fuckery is the fifth highest ratings grabber of the quarter, bested only by (#4) WCNT's Hawaiian Shirt Dance Party Weekend, (#3) WYYP's Domestic Violence Awareness Bowl-a-Thon, which features white bowling balls with black rings drawn around each of the finger holes, (#2) WNGR's Smooth Jams Tuesday, which is alternately guest hosted by Dionne Warwick and Reginald Denny, and of course (#1), the invincible WTLP's Abortion Kickball.

Our staff has been together for nine glorious years, tearing up the airwaves here in Ithaca, New York. This is no small feat; we are market #281 and growing fast. Compelling, aggressive radio is what's kept us rated in the Top 15 here year in and year out.

This is technically my second go-around here in Ithaca; I was originally producing for Seth Moil, a.k.a. Cancer Gums. Seth is the only DJ I've met whom I would agree was a shock jock. He held contests where he encouraged listeners to shoot police officers, and he offered free bumper stickers to anyone who sent him at least fifty megabytes of child pornography. The FCC once fined him $35,000 when he accidentally referred to Janet

Reno as "cunt face" during an impromptu phone interview. Shortly after I joined the program, Seth was killed when his van was rear-ended by a drunk driver as he attempted to kidnap an eight-year-old.

The job of any radio show, whether it's so-called shock jocks like Henderson & AIDS or any lame Top 40 DJ, is to keep people listening. We do. No one is turning off their radios during our benchmark bits, such as having people with Down's syndrome do Scarface impressions, or when the interns play our special version of Russian roulette: each picks a tin of yogurt to eat, one of which has donkey semen mixed into it. Politicians and the media demean the creativity of what we do when they throw around the moniker of shock jocks. I defy any of these do-gooders to find something on the radio more compelling then our own Musical Dildo Chairs or Parkinson's Patient Testicle Shaving. Shock jocks? No, sir; whether you like it or not, we are indeed artists.

—Jim Norton, radio personality

NOT OKAY TO MAKE JOKES ABOUT:	STILL OKAY TO MAKE JOKES ABOUT:
GAYS	PEDOPHILES
ASIANS	FAT PEOPLE
BLACKS	WHITE TRASH
WOMEN	DONALD TRUMP
RUTGERS BASKETBALL TEAM	STRIPPERS
CATHOLICS	MIDGETS
JEWS	
MUSLIMS	
9/11 WIDOWS	
RETARDS	

PUBLIC RADIO: FUND-RAISING

You're drawn to the prestige and gravitas of public radio. That means you're always looking to cultivate innovative fund-raising skills. The Public Radio audience has been cannibalized by satellite radio, the internet, podcasts, and violent manga comic books, forcing you to beg for sustenance. You cannot slack, and must organize an annual pledge drive four to fifteen times a year.

This may help . . . actual notes swiped from an NPR staff "brainstorming session" to generate exciting new ideas for pledge drive premiums.

Covering News, Politics, Art, and Culture like an elegantly hand-loomed Ubangi ceremonial rug.

Pledge Drive Premiums Wish List!!!

* Day-to-day desk calendars featuring 365 ways your prevailing attitudes and behavior might unconsciously project latent racism

* Youth Up membership drive with hip, new Tote Bagz.

* Fresh Air fresheners?

* Thirty bucks and we'll make those Car Talk guys shut the fuck up for an hour.

* I'm Making a Difference sweater vests.

* 3-D Ira Glasses.

* Donor can call in and request his or her favorite fugue.

* Pledges of over $500 entitle the donor to have his/her long-winded and reflective tale of awkward inaction turned into a segment on This American Life.

* A bag of rice candy or some other junk for your adopted Asian baby.

* Too Hot for A Prairie Home Companion DVD

* Adult Film DVD 2-Pack: All Holes Considered + This American Pissfreak.

* A solemn promise that Marian McPartland's Piano Jazz will take it up a notch.

* For every $50,000 in pledges received, will execute one member of the Capitol Steps.

* For $300 in pledges, South African singer Johnny Clegg will play a concert in your town; for $200 more, he'll also bring Savuka.

* Pledges of over $500 entitle the donor to sniff Terry Gross's cardigan sweater.

* Brian Lehrer will leave facetious outgoing message on your answering machine.

* Crate + Barrel compost hutch.

* Fresh tarragon?

* Copies of 1001 Things a Dog Might Say to His Psychiatrist: The New Yorker Cartoon Collection.

* Sharper Image electronic chin stroker.

YOU READ THIS SOMEWHERE

Morning radio shows are the #1 reason unattractive people end up on billboards.

MOGULDOM 101: KNOW YOUR FORMATS

To be a radio mogul, you need to know the medium inside and out. Study this chart and make sure you can identify radio's programming formats.

	Modern Rock Radio	Urban Contemporary
Sounds Like (to Devoted Listeners)	Hard-hitting modern rock classics without compromise.	Blazin' hip-hop and reggaeton, with smoothed-out R&B.
Sounds Like (to Casual Listeners)	The last thing you'll hear before the roofies kick in.	Bragging, complaining, bass.
Prevailing Attitude	"There is an unstoppable Rock and Roll Revolution coming, immediately following this advertisement for TrimSpa X32."	"Our cum slang will always be one step ahead of the FCC."
Best Listened to When . . .	In your car, getting "pumped" to deliver pizza and Crazy Bread.	Flashing around money you don't have.
Who Is Buying Commercial Airtime?	Auto dealerships.	McDonald's.
Target Demographic	Dudes, bros, buds, homeboys aged 18–34.	People wishing to make and/or receive a shout-out.
Cons	Rocking too hard can aggravate old softball injury.	Fergie somehow accepted here.

Soft Adult Contemporary	Pop Contemporary Hit Radio	Country	Air America
All your favorite hits from the '70s, '80s, and '90s, with a softer edge.	The biggest hits of today, from the biggest superstars in pop music.	Good old American pop music with an unmistakable country twang.	The voice of liberal America, at last.
The relaxing swirl of nonfat frozen yogurt being dispensed into a sugar-free cone.	An index finger rhythmically tapping against the side of an empty skull.	Git'R Sung!	Al Franken awkwardly clearing his throat.
"If you can just make it through this song without calling that two-timing ex of yours, the healing can begin."	"We are totally going to be best friends, like, *forever!!!*"	"There is not a problem in the world that can't be solved by me running over it with my truck."	"Bush Lied, People Chuckled Self-Righteously."
Scrapbooking through a veil of tears.	For him: Waxing your chest and/or balls. For her: Throwing a cell phone at your father after discovering he couldn't book Shakira for your Sweet 16 birthday party.	Dragging someone behind your pickup truck.	Sitting in the passenger seat of Al Franken's Prius.
Lean Cuisine Solos.	Bioré Face Bags.	Whittling accessories.	Wavy Gravy.
Single women 28–45, covered in cat hair.	Teenagers, catty adult women, and their gay best friends.	Guys with two first names.	Liberals, conspiracy theorists, fans of Janeane Garafolo.
High suicide factor during drive time programming.	Loss of innocence. Inevitable discovery that most pop songs are written by intergalactic kill-droids set on lulling our planet into helpless submission.	Disillusionment upon discovering, after a laundry mix-up, these colors do, in fact, run.	Falling asleep behind the wheel.

SATELLITE VS. COMMERCIAL RADIO

Five years ago if you had told someone you were buying a satellite radio, they'd have looked at you like you had two heads, four assholes, and a clubfoot. To most people, the concept of paying for radio was as foreign as paying to take a shit. The only thing satellite radio had going for it was the hopes that the greed of regular radio (made apparent by its two-minute Rock Blocks mixed in with fifty-eight minutes of commercials) would force people to seek an alternative. Since its inception, satellite radio now boasts approximately twelve million subscribers with an average of 2.4 people per subscription. (This per-subscription estimate is obviously higher among Mexicans, where the average household boasts 65.3 listeners per subscription.)

One of the earlier concerns was the horribly thin talent pool available to the satellite companies. No one successful in commercial radio was going to run face first into this untested, technologically fallible abyss. Early on, the only takers were highly incompetent, disgustingly old or convicted pedophiles. Then slowly but surely, people who had become the backbone of commercial radio—both on the air and behind the scenes—abandoned it in the same hurried fashion one displays after fucking a fat girl in the bathroom at a party. The radio graveyard that was satellite radio suddenly became a thriving, progressive force in communications. Local radio stations with their shitty playlists and twenty-five square miles of coverage will soon be obsolete. A person can literally drive from New York to Los Angeles and listen to the same station without interruption (this aspect has been particularly important to people who drive excessively, such as over-the-road truckers and serial rapists).

The growth potential in satellite is virtually endless, especially now with portable, handheld units. Keep your eyes open for their new, aggressive marketing slogans: "FM Causes Cancer," "Regular Radio: What Are You, a Jew?" and "Satellite Radio—Because Commercials Are for Queers."

5 TV AND FILM

FACT: YOU CAN BE a best-selling author, a top editor-in-chief, or a radio star, but you'll still be recognized by fewer people than the friend of the main guy on *Yes, Dear* if you don't make it on the big or small screen.

POSING STYLES FOR THE PAPARAZZI

The paparazzi killed Princess Di, embarrassed Jude Law's penis, and showed us where Britney Spears's babies came from. As a people, they're heartless, opportunistic, and vile. However, if you know how to play them, the paparazzi can solve as many PR problems as they create.

Most celebs strike generic poses as they angle for attention on the red carpet. To create a deafening buzz, you must be prepared to think like a true original.

PROBLEM: YOU ARE CONSIDERED TO BE A STUPID IDIOT.

Carry a book and wear glasses to *all* Hollywood hotspots. Open and "read." Fire away, a-holes!

PROBLEM (WOMEN): YOU'RE CONSIDERED OLD AND HAGGARD.

But are you flexible, Madonna? Do some yoga in people's faces. "If I were old and haggard, Mister Paparazzi, then how could I rest my calf on your shoulder with my head thrown back in girlish abandon? *The answer is I couldn't!*"

PROBLEM: YOU ARE CONSIDERED TO HAVE DONE A BAD JOB IN A VERY BAD MOVIE.

Pick a classic stage character and arrive in costume, monologue-ing. Guess who can't act now, bozos?

PROBLEM (WOMEN): YOU ARE CONSIDERED TO BE A MINDLESS SLUT.

Marry a gay dude. Stare lovingly up at him. *Click! Click!* Problem solved. Lay low for a while, divorce, and screw whomever you want again.

If you revere the sanctity of marriage and would like to avoid a false legal commitment, you have another easy option at your disposal: Go on a luxury rehab with a pool. Wear virginal white upon release and carry designer water bottles full of Ketel One.

Last option: Adopt African/Asian kids, tote them around, take on some political speaking engagements. Slut no more!

PROBLEM: YOU HAVEN'T WORKED IN A WHILE.

Arrive with the kind of hairstyle people can't help but comment on, then explain repeatedly that it's "for a part" that you're not yet "at liberty to discuss." Get your assistant to start a rumor about an upcoming Scorsese film that just might be the reason behind your purple dreadlocks. Also get fat and say that's for the film, too.

Film Actress To-Do List

✓ Get surgeon to move breasts up to shoulders.

✓ Become blonde, star in a legitimate film with the word "American" in the title. Play a sexually ravenous but troubled teen/cheerleader/arsonist.

✓ Hire Pellicano to destroy photos, negatives, and photographer who took pictures of you naked with pet mastiff back in the early '90s.

✓ Get Tom Ford to chew on earlobe.

✓ After first big film, lowlight hair and become brunette for two months to demonstrate lack of vanity.

✓ If popularity is waning, cry in car in front of paparazzi.

POWER SENTENCE: "It's just annoying that sometimes I can't even shop in peace."

ACTORS! MODELS! COMEDIANS! SUPERSTAR NOVELISTS! TIPS FOR CONQUERING BOREDOM WHEN YOU'RE TALKING TO YOUR MANAGER OR AGENT AT A PARTY

1   Drinks, drinks, drinks. Free, free, free.

2   Fake laughter, all around. Laugh at anything and everything. When in doubt, laugh.

3   Nod enthusiastically and say: "Right, right, right . . ."

4   If talk seems dark, shake head. You can say: "I guess you never know with these things."

5   Smoke cigarettes; cancer will be less painful than this silence.

6   Kill time by summarizing an epic novel you once read, milking each plot twist.

7   Tell a wacky audition (book reading, gig, et cetera) anecdote.

8   Debate about a popular TV show—is it good or *isn't* it? Get to the bottom of it!

9   Industry gossip. Got any? Any will do! Go! As long as it takes place "on set" or involves someone who's IMDb-able, you'll be fine.

10 Compliment them on their suits and hair gel.

11 Tell yourself: "These guys are my friends. These guys are great. This is a great match, me and them."

The whole time in your head you're doing Sudoku. It's on the walls of your mind. You're just adding numbers, floating in space.

SAMPLE AGENT-CLIENT PARTY CONVERSATION FLOW

"*How good is Lost, huh? How nuts is American Idol this season? Isn't it crazy that So-and-So got eliminated? What shows are doing well right now? What's the best show of all time, in your opinion? How 'bout yours? And how 'bout yours? Ahahahahahah! Good one! Right, right, right. Did you hear about the midseason replacement of that actor on that new sitcom? What?! Yes! Ouch. I know! That would be tough. Hey, how intense is The Wire? Soooo intense, right? Ahahahaha. Bad joke. Ahahaha. Bad joke, haha. Wow, that's obscure TV trivia. Dude, you know crazy obscure TV trivia. Hahahahahaha. You want another drink? 'Nother drink?*"

Film Actor To-Do List

✓ *Try to be from Australia.*

✓ *Marry dependable woman with thin brown hair who doesn't mind talking about acting career and will double as manager.*

✓ *Get in independent film and play ~~drug addict~~ ~~Jew~~ ~~fag~~ (Muslim.)*

✓ *Go to Sundance, Slamdance, Slamslamdance, and slamslamslamdance.*

✓ *Get mention of cheekbones and eyes from one of the following: A. O. Scott, Manohla Dargis, and/or that fat smelly blogger.*

✓ *Get signed to agency. Divorce wife.*

✓ *Go out with Sienna Miller a couple of times but DON'T GET TOO CLOSE.*

✓ *Marry someone from Christchurch, keep her there, and make sure she never leaves New Zealand.*

SIDEBAR PROJECT:
SPREADING GAY RUMORS

It's important to appeal to gays because lots of them work at CAA. It's crucial to hint that you are attracted to them. Here are some tips:

1   Kiss gay guys on the cheek when saying hello and good-bye. (Go for the lips if you can handle it.)

2   Wear crotch-enhancing jeans and tight tees. Keep hair boyishly messy and cute.

3   Roll your eyes to your gay agents when your girlfriend leaves the room.

4   Perform in a musical, befriend chorus boys, go to gay bar once or twice with them.

POWER SENTENCE: "It was hard to kiss another guy on camera at first, but I'm an actor. Of course, my wife was cool with it; she totally understood. In fact it turned her on. She is my life."

YOU READ THIS SOMEWHERE

Jessica Simpson and Ashlee Simpson are related by blood—the two are sisters!

HAIR AND MAKEUP PEOPLE: ARE THEY YOUR FRIENDS?

Any A-lister knows that perceived humility is an important trick. Part of this is pretending to be friends with your agents and managers, certainly—but is it required that you also pretend to be friends with hair and makeup personnel?

The answer is yes.

Hairdressers and makeup artists can be exhaustingly similar—a revolving door of gays and Botoxed semi-beauties with strong tans and in perpetually bad relationships—but you must pretend their small, dysfunctional personal lives excite you. Set aside a couple of moments. Memorize their names. Try your best to remember their individual stories (Sara is the one whose ex-boyfriend is stalking her, Gary is the one whose current boyfriend is after him, and Jordana is the one who just had to put a restraining order on her high school sweetheart). Try to remember who's into Botox and who prefers instead to advocate Restylane. Confide in them that you yearn for the days when you, too, were worried about things like your dad's health care or finding someone to look after your children. This makes them feel understood and valued . . . and then your hair and makeup will look nice!

These beauty professionals will, of course, try to bond with you as much as is humanly possible in the course of a hair or makeup sesh, and will slip you their personal business cards in the hope you'll request them on future jobs. Their fantasy is to go with you everywhere . . . to fly with you . . . to be as indispensable to you as your salary would be to them. Fair enough, Whatsyourname! If you feel ready, go ahead and request your favorites. Jennifer Aniston's longtime hairdresser knew her hair incredibly well and not because she'd been bouncing around from one pair of scissors to the next. It was because she made a choice and committed to that choice. As a result, her hair was finally understood in a way it never had been before. (Fifteen-minute cry break allotted.) Likewise, if you decide to settle down with a particular hairdresser, he or she should have the intense, unspoken vibe of: "I want to *know* your hair." Then you just pretend to be their friend for a couple decades to keep that flip from floppin'!

WRAP PARTY VISUAL CUES

How important was your project to the people who funded it?

Monitors playing clips of show	➔	You make Mommy and Daddy very proud.
Anything in carved ice	➔	Show was renewed . . . *yesterday.*
A-list celebrities on hand	➔	"Would you like a little money with that money?"
Open bar at hot spot	➔	Hopes are high.
Open bar at dive bar	➔	Bye, old friend!
Pizza delivered on set	➔	Congrats on a terrible job completed.
Cracker Jack box with name in Sharpie, tossed on desk	➔	Avoid referencing this project.

FILM CRITIC: WHAT TO SAY WHEN PR CALLS AFTER THE SCREENING AND THE MOVIE SUCKED

"May I interest you in some of my opinions on other subjects?"

"How can anyone put a value on a movie on which thousands of people have toiled so long and so nobly. One might as well choose from among one's children. [start weeping]"

"What, me? I'm a sad, sad old man. I have nothing to give. Nurse! Turn me over."

"Your hair smells great. Let's forget about the public part and talk about the relations."

"It was exactly one hundred minutes long."

CLASSIC COMPORTMENT AT THE SCREENING/PREMIERE OF YOUR FILM

As a high-profile creative force, all eyes will be on you at your film premiere or screening. The way you're perceived—your body language, your behavior, the noises you make—will be linked with the public's perception of your work.

Behavior to Avoid

No **patting yourself on the back.**

No turning around and **high-fiving the major investors** during moments of audience laughter or applause.

No **hand down pants** (own or plus 1) during love scene.

No **coughing loudly** during dialogue you dislike.

No **swigging from flask.**

No **playing dead.**

No leaning back and **covering face with hands.**

No **reading a book**—*even the Bible.* It will be taken as a lack of confidence in your project.

OVERHEARD AT SCREENING

"It was awful—a whole movie full of long takes of people walking for hours and saying nothing."

"It was transcendent—a whole movie full of long takes of people walking for hours and saying nothing."

Film Director To-Do List

✓ Get Dad to restrict trust fund. Work in a hard/humiliating job. (Note: you only have to do this for four to six months.)

✓ Write screenplay about job. Use credit cards to buy camera and to pay for shoot. (Important: You must MAX out your credit cards.)

✓ Marry high school sweetheart. Put her to work as PA.

✓ Release movie. Go to Sundance. Wear something sloppy to appeal to losers in the 20-35 heterosexual male demographic.

✓ Divorce wife, marry Nickelodeon actress or "Survivor" contestant with good body.

✓ Write second film. (Blocked? Try this: four men with a troubled past avenge their father. They are very close and cry and hold each other while they sob, but DO NOT HAVE THEM KISS.)

✓ Divorce actress, marry film starlet with credibility.

✓ Write third film about ~~drugs~~ ~~pedophile~~ (9-11).

POWER SENTENCE: "I maxed out my credit cards making my first feature."

YOU READ THIS SOMEWHERE

DVD packaging was initially designed to keep other people out of a DVD. Protecting the DVD from the consumer who purchased it was an unintended result.

From the Desk of... *Fred Armisen*

What does a movie producer do exactly? I wanted to find out for myself by sitting down and interviewing a working producer on the set of a real movie. For anonymity purposes, I am using the name "producer."

Fred Armisen: Hi! Thanks for agreeing to do this.

Producer: I've been insanely busy with this film. The hours are crazy. I was here at five in the morning!

FA: Wow. Why so early?

P: To be here. Oversee. Watch the crew set up. Oversee the setup.

FA: And do you tell them to change anything if you see something you don't like?

P: I try to stay out of their way. I mentioned something to the camera crew once and they ignored me pretty aggressively.

FA: So explain your job to me. I'm not quite sure what a producer does.

P: A lot. A lot. I was here at five a.m. It's crazy.

FA: Did you finance this movie?

P: Oh my god, no. That's the studio.

FA: Do you help create the artistic vision for the film?

P: No, the director and writers do that. I leave it to them.

FA: So are you more like a representative? Maybe of the studio?

P: No, the studio won't talk to me, so they send their reps for that. I do the grunt work. Watching decisions being made. Being made aware of the changes. I mean, changes happen in a split second. It's nuts.

FA: What does that mean? "Watching decisions being made"?

P: If two people are having a heated discussion, say the writer disagrees with how the movie is being shot or an actor wants to change his lines, I stand very close to the conversation. I cross my arms and look down at the floor like this *[he demonstrates]*.

FA: And then?

P: When a decision is made, I sigh and continue looking down. Then everyone goes back to work. It can get dramatic for sure.

(A second producer walks up. She is the coproducer.)

FA: Hi! So you're a producer on this too, huh?

Producer #2: Yeah, it's been total insanity. I flew in last night at eleven-thirty and had to be here at five!

P#1: *[Jokingly]* Poor baby! Let me give you one of my famous back rubs.

[He gives her a back rub.]

P#2: That is *so good!* Nice. Anyway, yeah. It's been a lot of flying back and forth.

FA: Talking to the studio?

P#2: Just. Crazy stuff. There's a lot of. They just want. It's too insane to get into it. I have to go back today. Then back tomorrow.

FA: I'm still a little unclear as to what you do.

P#1: We end up having to play good cop/bad cop a lot.

P#2: When stuff gets tough it's like, okay, we're going to have to play good cop/bad cop to get results—oh my God, that feels so good!

P#1: You're my widdle baby! We work very well together.

FA: Did you guys pitch the movie to the studio?

P#2: No, no, no. The writers and director did that. They were great in the room. So cool.

FA: I see. What is a typical day like? What did you do yesterday, for example?

P#2: So much stress! We got picked up at four-thirty in the morning.

P#1: They set up the video monitors for us.

P#2: And we sat and watched the feed. With headphones. All day.

P#1: They gave us these baseball hats at the beginning of the shoot.

FA: Cool. Black!

P#2: And check out these chairs.

FA: Oh yeah, it's got your name on it.

P#2: It does? I didn't even notice! I have been so *swamped!*

[A production assistant announces a meal break.]

P#1: Dude, it is so great to meet you. Sorry I am so distracted, there's a lot of stuff going on right now. Talk soon, okay?

P#2: Super crazy day, Fred. Bye!

I stayed for some of the shoot. It was a scene where a nervous man is looking through the personals of a newspaper. The producers looked very intensely into the video monitor, resting their chins on their fists.

                    Thank you, the end.

                    — *Fred Armisen, actor.*

From the
Desk of...

*L. Krafft**

We all get into these things differently. In my case, I had always promised my mother that I would bring her to the Emmys as my date. Of course, that was usually after she loaned me money. And I usually wrote on basic cable shows that featured strippers, whipped cream, Jenny McCarthy, the Barbi Twins, or any combination thereof, so what were the chances? Then I got a job on a hip political satire and the chances were good enough. We ended up with a nomination. The first thing I thought was, "Now what can I use to grease the wheels of that sweet, long-running money train?" The second thing I thought was, "I guess I could start promising my father I'll take him to the Oscars or something. Work the other angle?"

The first thing your mother will announce upon arriving at the red carpet is that it looks like everyone's wearing a bridesmaid's dress. Your favorite sighting will be the actress who always plays a very dignified wife or high-status patrician on TV and in movies (I don't want to give names, but she may have played the snoot with a soul in such hits as *The West Wing, Six Degrees of Separation, Le Divorce*, and many others). When she raises her arm to wave to a friend, point out to your mother that illuminated by the hot, dusty sun streaming through the front windows of the Shrine Auditorium is the most incredibly long underarm hair ever to be housed in an armpit. Really long. Unkempt if you will. Mesmerizing. Transcendent.

Once the show begins, even if you are pushing forty or something, which I'm not, but some might be, your mother will want you to behave yourself and not whisper. If you, say, lose in your nominated category and decide to go out and get a drink, she will chastise you impatiently—because, after all, the Aaron Spelling tribute is coming up. When you reply that you don't care, she'll remind you that you used to . . . you used to care.

Go out if you must. Get your silly drink. Hell, sneak a drag on a friend's cigarette. But when you get back to your seat, be prepared for your mother to be upset. She will hiss in her best stage whisper, "Well, I hope you're happy. You missed Charlie's Angels."

After that, the mad rush to the Governor's Ball. It will be faintly reminiscent of that last rooftop helicopter taking off during the fall of Saigon, only instead of hands desperately pushing children toward safety, it will be celebrities desperately pushing toward the bar, toward the celebritinis with the punny names. Push your sweet mother who spent thirty-six hours in labor with you forward! Push her forward!

The true celebs use the Governor's Ball only for a quick respite before speeding off to the real parties, leaving only the beginners and hangers-on. After staying for the full, leisurely meal, there will be another, quieter frenzy where your mother will sneakily pocket any and all prospective memorabilia to distribute to your nieces and nephews. It is not unlike when General Lee surrendered at Appomattox and General Grant had to order his men not to steal everything from the house as a memento. Not unlike it at all.

Ever feel lonely? Don't answer. Wait until you're sitting in the back of a limo with all your co-workers stroking their girlfriends/wives' backs or knees and whispering in their knees while your mother loudly asks if your girdle binds or if it's one of those newer, more comfortable ones? Your mother is a lady, it's just that the night has been long and the shoes have been tight. Ride it out.

Your mother will trudge up the hill to the after-party with a look of grim determination unwitnessed since Andersonville Prison stopped offering refills on bread crusts. Remember Andersonville Prison from the Civil War? Infamous Confederate prison? Take a moment to wonder what's up with you and all these military references. Once at the party, your mother somehow finds the one other parent there, quickly bonds, and together they beat a quick retreat back to the hotel.

You will remain behind, feeling vaguely and strangely guilty. Sit in the corner, have a drink. Sneak a cigarette. Your mother's gone, no one's going to tattle on you. Watch the couples all around you. You've done this before. Maybe it was the prom. Maybe it was a recent wedding where you were invited without a guest only to find that the one other single person at the reception is the aged, friendly priest and he doesn't feel like dancing.

Reflect. Your mother was your Emmy date. Information that others will respond to in weeks to come with a squeal and the declaration that "That is so cute!" And you will nod. It was so cute. Your mother was your Emmy date.

— *L. Krafft, television writer*

* Due to contractual restrictions: If you want to know which political humor show brought Laura Krafft to the Emmys, you're gonna have to IMDb her. Think of it as an elaborate name-drop scavenger hunt.

MAINTAIN GRACE AND POISE AT SWAG EVENTS

- Big smiles to all cameras with item in tow.

- Try not to have grabby look in your eye when you reach for and pull items to you.

- Don't take too much; make sure every pseudo-star gets his/her share.

- Remember to co-opt the term "free shopping" in order to make what you're doing seem more classier.

- No sighing: "Isn't it crazy we're getting all this free shit when the people who need it most go without?" If it makes you feel better, you're talking about $300 moisturizer, which no one needs.

- Don't think of yourself as an insignificant pawn in a massive marketing game—it's like looking over the edge when you're walking along a treacherous cliff.

- If there's only a single pair of size 2 jeans, generously offer them to the fattest girl. This will hammer home that you're a size 0.

- Remember: one paparazzi pic of you in any swag item equals major sales, so you're owed thousands of luxury goods you'll enjoy privately in your high-security mansion.

- If free shopping event is particularly high-end and newfangled swag taxes apply, do not calculate tax on site with your huge calculator that has a loud printing function.

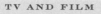

From the Desk of...

Andrea Rosen

In order to dominate as a commercial actress, you must be able to channel whatever f'd up thing is going on in your life, whatever murky moody mood you're feeling, into approachable friendliness.

You've Gotta Want to Book It

Helpful tips to get yourself into that winning head space:

> While in the waiting room, fake a smile so that you trick your body into releasing endorphins.

> Engage in some flirty texting. Eat sugar. Don't cry.

Motivational thoughts to help you get the job:

"If I book this commercial . . ."

1. "All of my exes will see it, making it impossible for them to ever forget about me. Just when I've finally fallen off of their radar, and they're curled up with their newest love, watching *Shark Week*, I will POP back into their world . . . I'll be ecstatically eating chocolate, knowingly wagging my finger at my dumb TV husband 'cause he didn't use the right detergent, sitting in a conference room pretending to be a Business Lady who understands how imperative it is that we switch to FedEx/Kinko's . . . Like a recurring nightmare I will stay with them. Like a fly you just cannot kill. I will linger for as long as the commercial runs."

2. "All of those guys who wouldn't go out with me 'cause they "just weren't feeling it" will regret it, 'cause they'll see how approachable and friendly I seem. How well lit I am. How perfect my hair looks and how pressed my wardrobe is. And then what'll they feel? Maybe they won't feel 'it,' but I'm certain they'll feel something. A tinge of regret? Definitely, maybe."

Make It Up

- Wear lots of makeup.

- Under-eye cover-up: Don't just cake it on, spackle that shit on.

- Powder: Anti-shine and anti-frizz are your new BFF's.

- Lips (ladies!): The shine doesn't come from your je ne sais quoi, it comes from your glossy lips.

- Eyes: If you don't curl your eyelashes, you must not want this job. So curl them!

- And lay that mascara on Alan Thicke.

And speaking of eyes, you must have them and use them and bat them a lot. If you have big eyes, that's good. Keep them big. If they are small, open up, sisters and brothers, make them as wide-eyed and engaged as humanly possible. (Note: A feeling of pure terror can elicit this same excited look. So think of something bloody, e.g., accidentally chopping your favorite person or pet with an ax, and you'll be golden).

Dress Vanilla

The world of commercials is idyllic, easy on the eyes, midwestern, regular and medium, and usually Republican. It's always 70 degrees and sunny with a light breeze. What you wear reflects this idea.

Nonthreatening attire		Threatening attire	
• Pastels	• Snaps	• Black	• Dangling earrings
• Floral Prints	• Small earrings	• Stripes	• Ninja suit
• Buttons		• Zippers	
		• Turtlenecks	

Here is a key to decipher what kind of outfit to wear:

When your agent says: "You are auditioning for the role of . . ."

"casual mom"	=	Old Navy
"hip casual woman"	=	Old Navy
"business casual woman"	=	Express
"casual woman"	=	Old Navy
"hip girl"	=	Urban Outfitters

It's important to look neat and clean even if you feel like a dirty and desperate, crazed and overwhelmed mess.

In Conclusion

Be fake, but don't act fake! And remember to have fun!!!!

If you do everything we've described, then you can totally *dominate,* and make billions, and eat pâté for breakfast, lunch, dinner, and snack. Get ready to be recognized. Because soon you will hear the words "You look really familiar" at least once a month.

— *Andrea Rosen, commercial artist*

TEN TV SHOWS THAT CHANGED OUR SOCIETY

1 **LOST.** It's *Gilligan's Island* meets *Baywatch* meets *The Twilight Zone*. Beautiful-bodied plane crash survivors, along with a token fat guy, deserted on a tropical paradise encountering unsolvable mysteries perfect for series longevity. There are obvious problems with the show, such as Matthew Fox's permanent two-day five o'clock shadow. Maybe he salvaged his beard trimmer, a.k.a. Miami Device, in the wreckage? And what's that fucking Hobbit doing in an American TV show? Hadn't we seen enough of him and his *Lord of the Rings* cast mates male bonding and crying like schoolgirls at the Oscars to be through with it? In a post–9/11 world, *Lost* is classic escapist sci-fi fantasy, sort of like *Star Trek* but different in every way.

2 **THE SOPRANOS.** Now we know that Italian-Americans do more than just eat spaghetti and kill people. They eat spaghetti, kill people, and then talk about it with a shrink afterwards. This TV show opened up a whole new world in TV show programming. It was the first show that said TV could be artful and serious without being hosted by a British fop in a leather chair.

3 **AMERICAN IDOL.** Alexis de Tocqueville has been reborn in the form of Simon Cowell. A shrewd chronicler of the American Mystique. Or is that Betty Friedan? Without *American Idol* we'd never have seen Paula Abdul's cleavage. Without *American Idol* Broadway would have no third-, fourth- and fifth-tier replacements for their national tours. *American Idol* is truly an American institution, right there alongside the death penalty and Scientology.

4 **OPRAH.** Look out, Jesus, there's a new Messiah in town and she's got a talk show, and a magazine, and a book club. Her name is Oprah Winfrey and she's here to save the world. Oprah is moral and upstanding. She introduced the phrase "Random Acts of Kindness" into the cultural lexicon. She's charismatic, whip smart, and rich as fuck.

5 **FRIENDS.** If only every apartment in New York City could look like that. If only we could all have friends like that. If we all had friends like that, then most of us would know Brad Pitt and Vince Vaughn. That's cool! The best thing about *Friends* is that it led to *Joey*. Can you imagine a world without *Joey*? We can. We can very easily.

6 **CHAPPELLE'S SHOW.** More known for the prodigious meltdown of its eponymous star than the show itself, *Chappelle's Show* set a new standard for self-destruction. It used to be, "Can you believe that Shelley Long left *Cheers* after only five seasons?" Now it's, "Can you believe that Dave Chappelle fled the country under a shroud of secrecy and hid in Africa while an entire network went down the tubes?" Shelley, you're off the hook.

7 **24.** We like this show because it shows that black people are really powerful in this country. More things happen in these 24 hours than is humanly possible, but who cares? There are beautiful people saving the world from destruction on a weekly basis. It's *Lost* (beautiful people) meets *Oprah* (saving the world) meets *Chappelle's Show* (destruction).

8 **THE GILMORE GIRLS.** They dance, they cry, they drink red wine, they talk about men, even though they love them, but guys are SO frustrating, and they fight but they always make up because they love each other so much and we love them so much and we love growing old with them and we love curling up in a blanket with a pint of Chunky Monkey and a vibrator and spending an evening with the Gilmore Girls.

9 **ACE OF CAKES.** Duff Goldman, TV's baddest-baker slash ex-graffiti artist, bakes with a team of punk rock assistants. They're more like a band than a bunch of lame people into pastries. Goldman uses drill saws and blow torches to assemble cakes so you know two things: one, he must have a huge dick; and two, he also likes to bake.

10 **JACKASS.** It's like looking at pictures of people with elephantiasis. This is the new freak show for our time. Our personal favorite is the paper-cut episode.

TV Actress To-Do List

✓ Botox entire face and neck until it is as smooth as a Corningware bowl. (Important: Be sure to leave eyes and mouth free for acting.) When people accuse you of having work done, furrow the area between eyebrow and eye to show indignation, but then IMMEDIATELY GO TO DERMATOLOGIST.

✓ Look for a script with a lesbian kissing scene.

✓ Get hit show where you play opposite fat man and focus on acting attracted to him. (Use techniques from that fucking Meisner class.)

✓ Work on hit show for five years, until syndication.

✓ Ask for $2 million after season three.

✓ Become fat.

✓ Become thin again, write book.

✓ Become fat again.

✓ Become thin again, become sponsor for product that makes you thin.

✓ Become fat again.

✓ Become thin again, find aged film actor, marry him. (Important: Actor MUST have been divorced at least three times.)

POWER SENTENCE: "But nothing I have done compares to my work with _____ [name of charity]." (If unsure of charity, ask house cleaner.)

TV Actor To-Do List

✓ Hire dialect coach to perfect one of the following accents: Boston, Alabama, or David Letterman.

✓ Work on a five-minute stand-up routine. (Tip: talk about beer, Arabs, your first girlfriend, how much of a loser you were in high school, and be sure to say things are "gay" when you mean stupid or lame.)

✓ After show, flirt with female network execs (the women with big hips).

✓ Become fat and bald, get own sitcom.

POWER SENTENCE: [In Boston accent] "I'm a regular guy."

TV Exec To-Do List

✓ Lose artistic dream.

✓ Get perm.

✓ Believe that women are not good comedians, Mexicans are less evolved humans, and gay guys actually kind of deserved AIDS. (IMPORTANT: do not say any of these out loud to anyone.)

✓ Become attracted to women who have straightened hair, round chest spheres the size of rugby balls, and no noses. Only nostrils.

✓ Get eyelift.

✓ For job: Look and see what is number one, steal script, shuffle pages around, hire new cast.

POWER SENTENCE: "Get down there and blow me. Yeah, you heard me. No, I'm not joking. Suck my cock, bitch."

From the Desk of...

A. D. Miles

When I found out that the pilot I had done for Comedy Central had been green lit to go to series, my first reaction was to go online and start shopping for a boat. Not a yacht per se, but something that could comfortably sleep at least five other people and would look good with "SS Success" stenciled across the back. This giddy optimism was stoked even further by a network executive who told us that the network was very excited about our show. "In fact," she said, lowering her voice for effect, "this show is the network's third-quarter priority." Now, I wasn't sure what that meant exactly, but I suddenly felt like I should be looking at slightly bigger boats. How much does a helipad cost? Ah, fuck it, go ahead and add the helipad.

Of course, this delicious anticipation of my new life as a celebrity was interrupted by the actual production of the show itself. A tedious affair involving endless calls of "action" and "cut" that seemed to stretch on forever. And then there were reshoots. And some of those reshoots had to be reshot and just when I was about to start complaining that the success I had wanted for so long was now taking too long, the Martini Shot was up. This was it, the last shot of production. "Savor these last few moments of anonymity," I told myself. "That distant rumbling you hear? That's a poon parade heading straight for your apartment."

There was only one last order of official production business, the Wrap Party. This is a wonderful tradition where the producers loosen the purse strings and treat the hardworking cast and crew to a lavish party. There's an open bar where everyone gets drunk, backs are patted, and makeup artists make out with gaffers. Mind you, this is what happens on just a normal production. If the production being wrapped is *a third-quarter priority*? Well, I wasn't sure if you could fill Alaskan king crab legs with Ketel One vodka, but that level of extravagance certainly wouldn't have surprised me. I guess this is where the roller coaster ride I was on crested and began its dizzying descent back down to reality.

The very idea of a wrap party seemed to have caught our production manager by surprise. There was a scramble to find a bar that could accommodate a large crowd at the last minute. You know, someplace shitty. I laughed it off. This was probably some kind of misdirect so that the champagne Jacuzzis would be even more of a shocker. But when I arrived, there were no champagne Jacuzzis. There was only an overwhelmed bartender in a smelly dive bar telling everyone that "open bar" was well drinks and one appetizer off the bar menu. A network suit was there and made a point of saying, "It was so great working with you!" Really? "Great working with you" is a video iPod with my name engraved on the back, not a generic shot of vodka and a basket of chicken fingers. What was going on?

It could have just been a clumsy lack of planning. But our pathetic wrap party might have been due to the fact that by the time we finished production, the first few episodes of our show had already aired and the ratings were only slightly better than what might have been achieved by filming a bowl of fruit.

—A. D. Miles, actor

DEVELOPING A THICKER SKIN, HOLLYWOOD STYLE

You've been in Los Angeles for years, paid the best trainer, deepened your yoga practice, and made great strides, according to your therapist. And yet you still burst into tears when a D-girl says your characters are clichéd. Your body is hard, but you're soft inside, like custard stuffed into a coconut shell.

The only way to truly prepare yourself for the constant cruelty flung at you in Hollywood is to anesthetize yourself with a large dose of it. Herein, tips to getting, reading, and overcoming bad reviews:

- Do something worthy of harsh criticism. Load your film with unnecessary visual symbolism! Direct a remake of a European film and cast it with the stars of *The OC!* Remember that critics need something to fill their empty pages, so anything will do. Note: If you fail in your goal to make something truly bad, request it not to be screened for critics. This will anger them into writing bad reviews, no matter how good the film or your performance.

- Go directly to Google. Do not pass go. Set a Google alert for your name. Click on the links and read the whole reviews. Think of it as a bench press. Those aren't fun either, but they make you stronger.

- Now that you've read your criticism, show the world that you don't care about it. Make a list of negative words used to describe you or your work. Use the words to describe yourself on your MySpace page. Post your worst review on your fridge and throw a dinner party. Silk-screen the same review on a T-shirt and wear it to the gym.

- Stare at yourself in the mirror every morning for a week and criticize yourself. Does it still hurt? If it does, make more bad work and start again. If it doesn't, you have succeeded in building thick skin.

Pop Diva To-Do List

✓ Make sure your father works at a mega-church.

✓ Pierce labia.

✓ Get pussy-whipped boyfriend to buy Pro Tools.

✓ Find repressed homosexual hip-hop producer to write, arrange, record songs.

✓ Get them to sing along with you in headphones to make sure you are in tune. (Helpful tip: practice in a karaoke room.)

✓ Do ONE of the following activities to appear edgy. (Note: only do ONE and then STOP.)

    * Stand on table at Lotus bar.

    * Date obese rapper.

    * Go out somewhere in public with dyke.

✓ Break up with pussyboy, go out with record executive.

✓ Marry executive, get rid of piercing, get pregnant.

✓ Pose as Bettie Page.

✓ Secrets of longevity:

    * Study Madonna's "Ray of Light" phase or get someone to read you the lyrics.

    * If tape stops during show, pretend to sneeze or faint.

    * At age forty-three, take pictures with crotch spread open.

POWER SENTENCE: "I'm keeping it real on this album."

Male Pop Star To-Do List

✔ Join chorus, take tap and jazz dance classes, get involved with the "Personalities" Contemporary Choir group after school.

✔ Become straight or at least try to kiss girls.

✔ Research and purchase the best pot you can find, go to sound studio with it, hang out late with beat master (use proper terminology). Become his really, really, really close friend.

✔ Cover up musical theater mannerisms as much as possible with gangsta moves.

✔ Here's a great way to practice: Wet your pants and walk across the room. Walk like this all the time.

POWER SENTENCE: "Me and LL Cool J are, you know, like bruthas."

A CAREER IN ENTERTAINMENT

1 year: 80+ MySpace friends.

4 years: "You look familiar . . . did we go to high school together or something?"

10 years: Someone recognizes you, cites project you weren't involved in.

15 years: Recognized outright, autograph and photo demanded.

6 THE INTERNET

WITH THE ADVENT OF THE INTERNET, socially awkward middle-aged guys living in their mothers' basements could suddenly connect with other losers across the world. Nerds became billionaires overnight. Charisma became obsolete . . . and Nick Denton became relevant.

EMAIL "POWER LANGUAGE"

The tone of a single email can make or break a career. Here are words and phrases that say: "I will destroy you on a business level."

Phrase	What It Communicates
Pls see attch'd	"I'm too busy to spell these words out for you, yet thorough enough to attach a comprehensive document or file."
DBNR	DBNR stands for: dictated but not read. As in: "I yelled something to my assistant who muddled through a retroactive transcription when I slammed my door shut for a nap." Slap a "DBNR" onto the bottom of your email and let it work its magic.
Keep in touch	"I wasn't exactly thrilled about this first contact. Please, do not feel free to contact me yet again."
I'm happy to do X, Y, Z if needed...	"I'm professional enough to offer that which you should not require of me."

Phrase	What It Communicates
...at your convenience.	"If you're adequately organized, 'your convenience' will be very, very soon."
...could use some clarification...	"You've been unclear so far."
Thank you for your patience.	"Be patient."
I look forward to speaking with you.	"You *will* respond."
OOT (Out of town)	"I am constantly traveling, due to international success. Would totally type this phrase out, but don't feel like it."
Will get that out by EOD...[End of the day]	"It's not ready (through no fault of my own, because I'm organized to the point of being on military time)."
Just checking in...	"Hey, bastard, nobody avoids me."
Good luck.	"Fuck off."
What's the ETA on that doc?	"Where the fuck is that fucking doc, you slacking piece of shit? How hard is it to do your frigging job, man? Seriously! Everyone else in here manages to get things in on time, but you, you're consistently dragging your heels."

THE ART OF THE VIIM (VERY IMPORTANT IM)

Like all major players, you know IM to be a crucial tool in the day-to-day domination of world media. You're so web-savvy, your towels were laser-monogrammed "WS" by something you rigged up through the internet. Every day, you use IM to handle important business. Polish up on your gameplay with the visual guide below—who knows—you might learn a new trick you could then toss into your expensive leather attaché case full of dirty tricks.

VIIM: HIRING

Use IM to hire prospective employees.

MediaMs
Is this Stan?

DoggiePue2
Yeah, y?

MediaMs
It was nice to meet u the other day. Ur hired.

DoggiePue2
4 real?????????

MediaMs
y!! need u to come in asap we r understaft.

DoggiePue2
wow awesum c u then!!!!!!!!111 :)

MediaMs
k. byeeee. . . .

VIIM: FIRING

Use IM to fire employees.

Mediaman
hey, btw

Loser
yea wats up

Mediaman
u know that project I put u on that every1s so hyped about?

Loser
yeah!

Mediaman
yer fired

Loser
r u kidding?

Mediaman
n

[Mediaman has gone offline.]

VIIM: CONFLICT MANAGEMENT

Use IM to manage conflict in the office.

HedHoncho

were you printing something a sec ago?

UnderLing

mm . . . y

HedHoncho

printer's 4 work related stuff

UnderLing

oh super sorry!!

HedHoncho

yea

UnderLing

thanks 4 letting me know, I wouldn't have known
if u didn't im

HedHoncho

np

UnderLing

k kewl

NURTURING FUTURE TALENT

Use IM to nurture relationships with top talent.

MrPower
u look cute 2day

FemaleIntern
oh

MrPower
yer skirt fits cute

FemaleIntern
oh ok :)

MrPower
i like the way it fits u

FemaleIntern
oh

MrPower
shirt 2 of coors!

FemaleIntern
ha oh

MrPower
u got the right body 4 it

FemaleIntern
oh ok

MrPower
yer hair is shiny/nice 2

FemaleIntern
k

MrPower
U like interning here so far?

FemaleIntern
Yeah it's been really gr8, learning a lot

MrPower
Good to hear. Just checking in.

EMAIL: POWER SIGNATURES

While the general rule of thumb is that "email signatures are for secretaries," a well-chosen quote can send a powerful message to your correspondent.

Do *not* quote the following personalities. Due to their extreme positions and divisive perspectives, they will serve to alienate your correspondent, rather than inspire respect.

UNQUOTABLES (TRAPS!)

Unabomber Theodore J. Kaczynski, Joan of Arc, Osama bin Laden, Janeane Garofalo, Hitler, Jim Jones, Pee-wee Herman, Dante, Sylvia Plath, Marilyn Manson, Timothy McVeigh, Mohamed Atta, Napoleon, Fergie from the Black Eyed Peas.

Unacceptable signatures

NO!   *"Anyone who sees and paints a sky green and fields blue ought to be sterilized."—Adolf Hitler*

NO!   "The victor will never be asked if he told the truth."—Adolf Hitler

NO!   "TO ME DEATH IS NOT A FEARFUL THING. IT'S LIVING THAT'S CURSED."—JIM JONES

NO!   "I shut my eyes and all the world drops dead; I lift my eyes and all is born again."—Sylvia Plath

NO!   "I DON'T JUDGE OTHERS. I SAY IF YOU FEEL GOOD WITH WHAT YOU'RE DOING, LET YOUR FREAK FLAG FLY."—SARAH JESSICA PARKER

NO!   "For where the instrument of intelligence is added to brute power and evil will, mankind is powerless in its own defense."–Dante Alighieri

NO!   *"Everyone has their different look. Will's got his knickers and crazy socks, and Taboo has his kung-fu wear. I have to think of words to put my style into. I would say kind of urban gypsy, because I collect things, accessories, from all over the world (Asia, Africa, Brazil), and that is definitely what, for me, helps make an outfit my own."—Fergie, Black Eyed Peas*

QUOTABLES

DO quote the following people, they are solid: Gandhi, Shakespeare, Maya Angelou, Nelson Mandela, Martin Luther King, Mother Teresa, Norah Jones, Winston Churchill, Abraham Lincoln.

Acceptable signatures:

YES!   **"We must be the change we wish to see."—*Gandhi***

YES!   *"We must use time wisely and forever realize that the time is always ripe to do right."—Nelson Mandela*

YES!   **"Let there be work, bread, water, and salt for all."** —*Nelson Mandela*

YES!   **"Do not wait for leaders; do it alone, person to person."—*Mother Teresa***

YES!   **"How important it is for us to recognize and celebrate our heroes and she-roes!"—MAYA ANGELOU**

YES TIMES 10!   *"I believe that every person is born with talent."* **—Maya Angelou**

YES!   **"LIFE LOVES THE LIVER OF IT."——MAYA ANGELOU**

YES!   "I WAITED TILL I SAW THE SUN / I DON'T KNOW WHY I DIDN'T COME . . ." —*NORAH JONES*

INTERNET MOGUL VOCABULARY CHECKLIST

When it comes to "the net" are you keyboard-crushingly, mouse-poundingly powerful? Could you be? Let's check.

How many of the following words do you already know?

TRAFFIC

UNIQUE VISITORS

STATS

SIDEBAR

BROWSER

URL

DOMAIN NAME

BOOKMARK

REFERRER

If you don't know any of these words, please turn to page 25, 55, 79, or 97 because you are too far behind on the internet. It would take you forever to catch up. And then, by the time you were caught up on some of *this* stuff, everyone else will have moved on to other crap you'd have to learn. It's just gonna be a real pain and hopeless.

YOU READ THIS SOMEWHERE

All joking aside, PayPal does need your info in order to properly update your account. Email all info to: scammypoo22394@hotmail.com.

From the Desk of...

Nick Denton

I was combing my eyebrows in the mirror when I felt a claw tap at my shoulder.

Whipping around, I saw nothing behind me yet heard that unmistakable, gravelly voice: "How would you like to become the King of the Internet?"

"I would! I would!" I exclaimed into the void.

"Okay," the terrible voice answered. "You can. But of course, there is a cost."

As if on cue, I heard a distant shrieking. Unperturbed, I answered, "I don't mind. Whatever the cost, I'm okay with it." Then I caught myself—just in time. "As long as you're talking about a moral or social cost, not a financial one."

A dark invisible nod filled the room. Then I heard that voice gurgle again, this time as if perched on my shoulder. No, closer than that—it was as though the voice were coming from within my own large-ish head. "It shall be so," the voice declared.

And then there was the most frightful silence I have ever known—pierced by the sound of my eyebrow comb clattering to the floor from my sweaty palm. "*Wait!!*" I called out, but it was too late—the voice, and the Prince of Darkness it belonged to, had left the room. There were so many questions I had wanted to ask: "How many niche blogs can one man create? When do I eliminate a weak niche blog from my niche blog stable? Is niche pronounced *nitch* or *neesh*?" And other questions about niches.

But those questions would all have to wait, for he was gone.

It didn't matter. Before I knew it, things were falling into place. My docile employees seemed willing to do anything for sweatshop wages. My personal photographer, responsible for documenting my attendance at various social events, seemed to discover a new "best angle" every day.

"How can I expand my empire, Dark Lord?" I asked one night, tossing pebbles out my window at Balthazar. "I'm King of the Internet, yet hunger for more. Show me the way!"

Again, I felt a claw clamp down on my shoulder, and the chilling disembodied voice cleared his throat. "Have you considered doing a book? Some publisher will probably pay you a shitload of money just to slap the Gawker name on the cover of a book."

"A book?" I scoffed. "I don't have time to write a book."

"Of course not," the Devil agreed. "Hire writers. Pay them nothing. You know, do your thing, Nick—do your thing."

And with that, he was gone—again leaving me bursting with unanswered questions. I called out into my enormous loft: "Should I avoid eye contact with these writers when we are at the same parties? How would that serve my cause, Dark Lord?" Alas, only an echo came back to me.

And yet the path had become clear.

—*Nick Denton, internet mogul*

THE ART OF THE URL

When you register a url for your site, avoid idiotic pitfalls. Your url should be short, memorable, and easy to spell. For this reason, four-letter domain names are in high demand. A four-letter word is nice. Even four-letter swear words (*fuck, shit, cunt, tits, cock, fuck, dick, twat, poop, crap, wank, slit, clit, butt, nuts, hole*) may fetch a high price in the Adult Entertainment genre if that is your lucrative area of focus. The fourteen-letter url hasn't caught on yet, but that doesn't mean it won't.

More rules of the internet highway:

Avoid confusing spelling. Urls such as: DatzWatZup.net, ReawlCooleGurrllie. org, and Gawdzooques.com will only get you into trouble with impatient web users. If you have to explain the spelling every time you verbally relay the url, you've created an irritating scenario for yourself and all involved.

Avoid lots of spelled-out numbers. Urls such as: OneThousandThreeHundred EightyTwo.com, ThirteenMillionZillionBillionAndOne.org, and NineHundred ThousandBajillionAndFive.net make for horrible business, as do TwentyOne ThousandThreeHundredAndThirtyTwo.com and EighteenThousandFour HundredAndTwelve.com.

Avoid using your name. Unless your name is James Smith, leave your family background in the distant background. No one wants to guess around for the correct spelling of Kalinowska. And no, the spelling of Galifianakis *isn't* "instinctive," Mr. Confident!

THE BIGGIES

To make good money online, you must be one of the most highly trafficked sites in the world. Chances are, you've seen the following prestigious websites. What makes them so powerful? Answer in your head.

MSN

GOOGLE

YOUTUBE

MYSPACE

YAHOO

FACEBOOK

ITUNES

8TH STREET LATINAS

MAKING MEANINGFUL CONNECTIONS WITH (OTHER) INTERNET MOGULS

Making friends in the online world is as easy as typing a compliment and clicking *send*. Most of the moguls who dominate the internet, though successful, were once exceedingly unpopular, and/or fat, and/or pizza-faced dorks. That's still how they feel inside, even if they're now able to wine and dine with a flock of followers who are drawn to prominence, wealth, and success like moths to an LCD monitor. Though you might have to contend with some initial nerd ego, the internet mogul's sensitive core is not difficult to penetrate.

Write an email that says: "Enjoyed your site today. Would love to grab a drink sometime." BAM. That's it. They'll almost certainly respond, in the hopes that you'll erase years of painful rejection by continuing to enlarge the scope of their newfound glory.

INTERNET IMPRESARIO: ATTITUDE

If you work in the internet, your attitude should be quite lofty. Chances are, you understand how the online world works better than 90 percent of the people you will encounter in day-to-day life. Talk down to them, use *au courant* buzzwords they'll never understand, reference internet squabbles and viral trends they may be unfamiliar with, and—whatever you do—do *not* offer to fill in the blanks. It's easy to be an expert when everyone else is so ignorant. In a weird way, the internet is like a high school where you're the captain of the football team. (In this analogy, "50-somethings" are "cheerleaders on roofies.")

UNDERSTANDING YOUR PLACE
IN THE BLOGOSPHERE

Weblogs (a.k.a. blogs) can be found all over the World Wide Web, as online journals filled with the author's daily reflections, favorite hyperlinks, photographs of the Apple Store, and spirited dialogue about everything, from the new Radiohead album to the new Thom Yorke album.

If your blog becomes a "destination," you will: befriend celebrities, receive swag, pocket advertising money, become privy to insider info, break stories, sell merch, impact elections, be covered by all other branches of media, and get a book deal—all the while wearing your favorite soiled pajamas. You will be a voice to be reckoned with in the American media landscape, a formidable brand, an indispensable source for whatever it is that you exclusively offer. Which brings us to an important point: What will you offer? Do you just kind of like to talk shit about people? That's fine, but it's important to know. A variety of blogs are out there, each serving its own unique purpose within the great blogosphere . . . specifically, what type of blogger are you?

LINKBOT

`http://nothingtosay.blogspot.com`

Just as robots express themselves with a series of high-pitched bloops and bleeps, some bloggers harvest the web and link to other people's published words as a surrogate for personal expressions of intellect, skillful writing, or "emotions." For example, to express his own moral outrage the linkbot might include a link to a *New York Times* editorial on his blog. Conversely, to express joy, the linkbot would simply link to a *video of a chimpanzee drinking its own urine*. When away from his computer, the linkbot is hooked up to a thick, metal tube that provides all necessary nutrients, just like in *The Matrix*.

CORE READERS: victims of carpal tunnel syndrome.
FAVORITE TOPICS: memes, stats, trends, charts, polls, Radiohead.

MOMMY BLOGGER

`http://mykidrules.typepad.com`

Most would agree that it's difficult to imagine anything more interesting than someone else's baby. Lucky for all of us, Mommy Bloggers take that idea and truly run with it, observing their baby's every finger twitch, eyelid flutter, or fontanelle ripple and recording them with lengthy and nuanced attention ordinarily demanded of an on-duty doctor in a coma ward. And it's all written in a prose style slightly less sophisticated than actual baby talk.

CORE READERS: other mommies, browbeaten members of extended family, cesarean fetishists.
FAVORITE TOPICS: miracles, blessings, chapped nipples, Radiohead.

`http://www.xanga.com/arentihot`

If, while researching telecom equipment pricing, an innocent typographical error causes you to accidentally query Google for "BARELY LEGAL + LIVE + WEBCAM + REAL DEAL," you're probably acquainted with Cam Girl bloggers. These enterprising young women are so bursting with a joyful eagerness to please that they can barely contain it within their tight midriff T-shirts and thong underwear. Cam Girls are characterized by their generous sense of virtual community, which they are happy to extend to anyone regardless of their age, physical attractiveness, command of grammar, or high-profile status on the federal government's list of known sex offenders. And in exchange, these otherwise thankless heroes of the blogosphere merely ask their fans help subsidize the cost of some basic necessities—rent, laptop computers, expensive panties, iPods, *One Tree Hill* DVD collections, diamond-studded clitoral piercings, vibrating eggs, et cetera.

CORE READERS: middle-aged men unfettered by society's fascistic sexual mores, producers at *Dateline*'s "To Catch a Predator," estranged father.

FAVORITE TOPICS: online poll—"Which thong underwear should I sleep in tonight?," Amazon.com wish list updated with new Radiohead album.

Tired of handing out your 9/11 conspiracy theory pamphlets to tourists visiting Ground Zero? Why not give your feet a much-needed rest and take it to the blogosphere? The web has several advantages over traditional means of spreading your political message. For one, each sensationally partisan argument, no matter how crazy-sounding, can be supported by a seemingly credible link to another, even more crazy-sounding political blog. And if your opinion turns out to be even too unsubstantiated for a personal blog, you can always delete it and deny ever posting the offending opinion to begin with.

Plus, instead of just wearing a button bearing a picture of Osama bin Laden or Hillary Clinton in the crosshairs of a sniper rifle, thanks to the web, you can post an image of Osama bin Laden or Hillary Clinton in the crosshairs of a sniper rifle, then animate in a bullet fired to your political enemy's face, over and over again. Then just wait for your comments section to fill up with angry detractors from "Religious Right Nutjobs" or "Crybaby Liberal Whistle Blowers." That's the political system at work.

CORE READERS: opposing party members, Homeland Security.
FAVORITE TOPICS: why we need to stand behind/impeach our president; the Middle East liberation/imperialist occupation; Radiohead.

http://snarkypants.blogspot.com

Often writing in the "royal we" and armed with only bravery and delightfully sardonic wit, the Deadly Snark is not afraid to launch a full-on preemptive assault of everything our culture holds dear—even if it means upsetting a few Dave Matthews fans. Only under the preternatural scrutiny of this blogger are we able to peel away the veil of the superficial and see that Paris Hilton is indeed a "skank," or that Jennifer Lopez could also answer to the name "J-Ho," or that, despite every bit of evidence to the contrary, Jared Leto is a "douche." Some might accuse these bloggers of enjoying a parasitic relationship with pop culture, mercilessly chipping away at those whose successes and charisma far outweigh their own, while hiding safely in the shadows of the blogosphere. But there is no doubt the Snark would gladly repeat all of his comments verbatim, directly to the faces of his celebrity targets, if only those celebrities would extend an invite to just one of their parties. Even as a +1 or something. But until the invitation comes, our poor, beleaguered pop culture desperately asks: Is there *anything* this snarky blogger truly enjoys? And the answer echoes back with a haunting: "Whatevs."

CORE READERS: 18–34-year-olds of average or below-average charisma, Jared Leto, you.

FAVORITE TOPICS: hipsters, scenesters, and other people enjoying a rich social life; the new, overrated Radiohead album.

While toiling away at their various day jobs, a select group of low-level working stiffs have found the courage to illuminate their working conditions by starting a blog on company time, then spending the workday anonymously posting about how cruelly they are being treated or how much blow lawyers snort. Details are often cleverly disguised to protect the author's identity. For example, in the world of the industry insider blogger, Condé Nast becomes "Condé Nasty," or a difficult boss is known only as "Chankles" or "Pig Cunt." Even if the author's writing technique is only about as good as Mommy Bloggers or People Who Believe in the Factual Existence of Angels, it doesn't matter—as long as the blogger has an important story to tell. And as long as that story includes intimate details about the sexual predilections of famous or powerful people.

Of course, recording these proprietary and sensitive workaday details comes with the risk of termination or blackballing, and many times the blogger is forced to literally take it in the ass for the sake of producing a compelling narrative. But these bloggers persist, knowing their only reward is Truth, and a lucrative publishing/television/film deal.

CORE READERS: junior literary agents, assistant editors, the *New York Times*.
FAVORITE TOPICS: being victimized, swearing revenge, Radiohead's private concert on your boss's yacht.

Champions of independent music and alternative music alike, music bloggers hold an exceptional amount of sway in both the blogosphere and record industry. By plying these bloggers with zero-cost premiums like concert tickets or MP3s from upcoming releases—the music industry equivalent of trinkets and glass beads—record labels have been able to generate serious buzz for their "low-interest" bands virtually for free. And even an easily forgettable new artist like Band of Horses can go from sounding "derivative of" to "reminiscent of" My Morning Jacket in the hands of the right music blogger. Sure, you'll always dread checking in at a concert venue and saying, "I think I'm on the label's guest list. It's under the name hiddentrack.blogspot.com," but think of the great blog post that concert will make.

CORE READERS: PR flacks, other music bloggers, "cool" dads.
FAVORITE TOPICS: why this was the worst year ever for new music (followed by your year-end Top 20 list); excitedly posting an MP3 by a new artist who is also prominently—and coincidentally!—featured in your Google ads; sly, knowing, and repeated references to owning the new Radiohead album months before its scheduled release date.

YOUR MUSIC BLOG NAME

☐ Is the name of your music blog a clever and obscure reference to a seminal indie band, e.g., largeheartedboy.com?

☐ Is the name of your music blog a clever, even more obscure reference to a relatively unknown indie band you incessantly evangelize and that, once famous, you will make unsolicited claims to have "been way into before everyone else," e.g., youaintnopicasso.com?

☐ Is the name of your music blog a smugly ironic and lazy preemptive attack against other cleverly named music blogs, e.g., clevertitlesaresolastsummer.blogspot.com? (In the blogging world, this technique is known as "taking the high road.")

If you checked any of the above you're well positioned to have a bunch of people link to you.

YOU READ THIS SOMEWHERE

Wireless internet providers are fast outpacing wireless phone service providers in the "providing a service that is often unavailable" sector.

Due to its vast size, the blogosphere can accommodate a seemingly infinite number of images of street people photographed with expensive camera equipment. And that's only good news for the legions of photobloggers online who post photo after photo of gritty, urban environments, fringe characters, blog events, and kitschy foreign billboards advertising American motion pictures, often without any accompanying commentary. Without the photoblogger, we might never know what a subway car crowded with computer programmers in Santa Claus costumes looks like. Or that, in Tel Aviv, *Wayne's World* was called *The Two Idiots*. Of course, with the advent of photo-sharing sites like Flickr, the photoblogger has been rendered nearly obsolete, but as long as there are black babies and costumed pets, the photoblogger's work is not done.

CORE READERS: people conducting a Google image search for "graffiti + ironic placement of."
FAVORITE TOPICS: homeless people, abandoned warehouses, dogs in tutus, Asian food, extreme close-ups of new Apple products.

`http://parkerisms.livejournal.com`

On the surface, the Aspiring Author is no different than any other online diarist, recording a detailed account of his daily adventures, however mundane. But look a little deeper and the differences begin to appear. Instead of writing "I walked to Jamba Juice," the Aspiring Author writes, "I perambulated to Jamba Juice." Every noun and verb is adorned with not one, but *several* modifiers. "I grabbed my ancient, withered Game Boy, placed it in my shiny blue fannypack, and hurriedly raced up the rickety stairs of my basement apartment. 'I'm coming, Mom!' I loudly intoned." The text practically leaps from the page and into your heart. This is no ordinary blogger. This is an untrained writer trying to attract the interest of the publishing industry, and doing so with gusto.

> **CORE READERS:** sites checking their referrer logs, ex-boyfriends googling author.
> **FAVORITE TOPICS:** other bloggers' book deals, the pros and cons of going with Xlibris.

`http://360.yahoo.com/imsosubtle`

Say you've stumbled across a new blog through one of your favorite message boards. As you're reading about the true adventures of a horny Martian who came to planet Earth to study human mating rituals, you begin to think to yourself, "Hmm . . . this Martian sure seems to love AXE Bodyspray." You might have been lured into an online advertising campaign disguised as a blog. It's more common than you'd think. Since the advent of blogs, clever advertisers have been using the medium to build online relationships with their customers. If you find yourself enthralled by the adventures of young, hip, offbeat, and adventuresome man or woman with an above-average interest in a particular consumer good, you're very possibly reading the work of an ambitious advertising copywriter rather than, as you previously assumed, the actual Mayor of Snickersopolis.

CORE READERS: other advertising agencies, industry trade magazines, Mormon teenagers.
FAVORITE TOPICS: extreme sports, "cool tunes on my portable MP3 player," the importance of antioxidants.

SPOTLIGHT ON MUSIC

MUSIC-RELATED CONTENT

Have you ever posted any of the following content?

- ☐ I Am Totally Losing My Shit Over the Newly Leaked Radiohead Album.

- ☐ Yeah, Yeah, I'm Probably the Last Blogger to Weigh In on <UNIFORMLY EMBRACED INDIE ROCK BAND FROM CANADA> but . . .

- ☐ This Glowing Post about MF Doom/Dizzee Rascal/Manu Chao Projects a Willingness to Support Genres of Music Outside of My Indie Rock Comfort Zone.

- ☐ Does Anyone Know Where I Can Get Radiohead Tickets? Seriously. I'm Stoked.

- ☐ Ryan Adams Did *What??!!??* What a Douche!

- ☐ Jack White Did *Huh??!!???* What a Maverick!

- ☐ The Latest Example of Why Michel Gondry is a Very Creative Video Director.

- ☐ I 100% Agree with <LINKED MUSIC BLOGGER>'s Latest Post and Here Is a Remarkably Similar Post to Prove It.

- ☐ I Know I Should Hate This New Paris Hilton/Kelly Clarkson/ Lindsay Lohan/Killers Single, But . . .

- ☐ Maybe I Jumped the Gun on That Whole "Grime" Trend in England.

The more you checked, the more unique visitors you deserve.

EDITORIAL RANTS/TOPICS FOR DEBATE

Place a check beside the topics you have posted rants on:

- ☐ The ridiculous number of bloggers with digital cameras who are ruining concerts for the rest of us by getting in the way of my digital camera.

- ☐ Pitchfork Media writes the worst record reviews and I should know— I've read every single one of them.

- ☐ Here is the solution to all of the RIAA's problems.

- ☐ Music blogging is not a crime!

- ☐ Why I will never buy another CD.

- ☐ Streaming vs. Downloading: Which is more boring?

- ☐ Why this Coca-Cola commercial proves <MAINSTREAM MUSICIAN> is a corporate whore.

- ☐ In defense of the Coca-Cola commercial featuring music composed by <RESPECTED INDIE MUSICIAN>.

- ☐ I do not have an editorial responsibility to my readers!

- ☐ Radiohead: the next Beatles? Or better?

Again, the more checks, the merrier.

MYSPACE: CONGRATULATIONS!
YOU, AS A PERSON, ARE A BRAND!

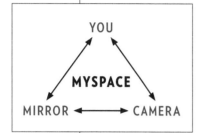

If you're huge on MySpace it's because you adhere to the #1 Rule: You love yourself. You *must* love, love, LOVE yourself. If you don't, you're dead, facedown in a blood-filled networking pool of losers. Do you feel super-intense about yourself? That each new day shared between you, your mirror, your camera is a gift?

If you only have 200,000 friends, it's time to get active! You need more. Here are some methods you can try to increase your friend stats:

1   Look in the mirror.

2   Take out camera, take a hundred pics (handheld).

3   Upload best.

4   Set camera timer, get in underwear, sit around.

5   Upload best to pics.

6   Write lists (#1 through 10): My Best Features, The Sexiest Things About Me as a Lover, My Biggest Accomplishments, My Endearing Vulnerabilities, The Famous People I Know . . .

7   Look at those lists.

8   Don't you see? They're the raw materials for your profile information.

9   Sit-ups. You should be doing a thou a day.

An infatuation with digital self-portraiture isn't enough. Being the best on MySpace entails upkeep in *several* areas. Here's a guideline.

FAQ: IS IT GOOD FOR YOU, AS A BRAND ON MYSPACE, TO . . .

Upload the maximum amount of photos to your pics section? YES

Photo checklist:

- ☐ Hot fan wearing your promotional shirt.

- ☐ You, somewhere elite/exotic.

- ☐ Family pic to show you're grounded.

- ☐ "Humbling" candid (you in front of a billboard for your upcoming project with caption: "Eek! My first billboard!")

Modify your template? YES

A custom template sends a message: "I, like all the other people who modify their templates on MySpace, march to the beat of a different drummer."

Watermark all jpgs with myspace url? YES

Fans that repost pix will not only promote your face *but also your precise location on MySpace.* Yay, more eyeballs, you ridiculous piece of shit!

Post media? YES

Your "media" includes a trailer for your upcoming movie. Also, you've made your MySpace–exclusive podcast available. It consists of you reading your MySpace fan messages aloud and "answering" them. Which consists generally of saying: "Yes, I *am* hot." And "No, I'm not god."

Blogger Star to-Do List

✓ Get called "Fatso" and "Fag" in elementary school.

✓ Learn HTML.

✓ Transmute Columbine-like feelings of murderous hatred for popular high school kids into an unquenchable love-hate obsession with celebrities.

✓ Create site, get waiter and valet friends to tip items to you about aforementioned celebrities.

✓ Find out something disgusting that Jeff Probst did, post it.

✓ Spend all day at The Coffee Bean eating cream-filled croissants and cappuccinos, collating tips, then write a long think piece about Nicole Richie.

✓ Begin dressing like Boy George or someone on "Project Runway."

✓ Acquire advertisers hungry for attention from MySpace Generation.

✓ Get pictures taken with celebrities that you write items about, thus becoming integral to their fame in a strange braiding of sycophancy, PR, and self-abnegation.

POWER SENTENCE: I am not a Trekkie.

7 FINAL PREPARATIONS

YOU'RE ALMOST THERE, CONQUEROR. By this point in the book, you've successfully:

- set goals

- reached goals

- alienated friends and family who were intent on "distracting you" from goals

- severed emotional/human response to being loathed by others

But you're not there yet. Not quite. Not only are we contractually obligated to fill at least fifteen more pages, but we have more to teach before we set you loose. In this final chapter, you'll learn how to recover from traumatic setbacks and discover other bits of wisdom thrown in like sawdust in a turkey.

The big remaining question: *How does one turn a failure into a success?* Failure is inevitable, after all. Politicians, actors, and businesspeople—we all do it. We fail constantly. Failure is a part of success. All you have to do is watch an old episode of *Date My Mom* to understand the immensity of this profound truth.

In media, it's crucial to be able to reposition a devastating failure into a positive event. But how?

YOU READ THIS SOMEWHERE

Prior to Google, NYC dating was just two people learning about each other as they went along.

HELP, I FUCKED SOMEONE WHO IS IMPORTANT TO MY PROFESSIONAL DEVELOPMENT

So. You got drunk at a work party and you fucked someone important, didn't you? It was a risky play, with high backfire potential. As the memory comes racing through your dehydrated mind, you must quickly consider next steps. Guess what doesn't count as a plan of action? Staring at yourself in the mirror as if at a stranger, all puffy eyes and handfuls of Advil, the fear of unemployment raging through your bowels . . .

Don't sweat it, genius. You can't afford to lose any more body fluids. It's time to reset the tone. Here's a to-do list for your next workday:

- Act more professional than ever. Use words like "sir" or "ma'am" to clarify proper boundaries have been restored.

- Start most sentences with: "In my professional opinion . . ."

- Avoid direct eye contact. (Certainly avoid a combination of eye contact and suggestive eyebrow-raising.)

- Do not whistle or sharply inhale when this party bends over.

- Announce marriage plans to a third party, via company email.

- Don't wear anything sexy. Nothing flashy or tight. Your fashion for right now should be monklike. Think flowing, and robes. You have a singular, almost religious business purpose.

- Man or woman, carry your briefcase at all times. Never let that leather handle fall from your tight clutch. This reminds people you would not fuck anyone in the career power pool because you are so ridiculously professional.

HAVING SEX LIKE A PRO

The next time you pull up to a "should I or shouldn't I" sex crossroads, subtly whip out this wallet-sized (if you fold it three times) cheat sheet to determine the right call.

FUCK OR FLEE?

→ YOUR BOSS

Fuck. An age-old strategy for self-promotion. Sleeping with the boss to get ahead has been in style—from when You-Know-Who Gave it up to The Big Boss to create a certain Son of Man, to when Mariah Carey gave it to Tommy Mottola to forge a music career. And the list goes on.

→ YOUR ASSISTANT

Fuck. We can hear what you're thinking.* "Sleep with my assistant? That's madness! Why would I choose a bedfellow who was down a few notches in the corporate ladder?"

Because sex can buy you loyal devotion. Played the right way, the assistant/lover will always be ready to do your bidding. Perfect if you want that coffee extra hot and that filing extra file-y.

→ YOUR HIGH-POWERED ATTORNEY

Flee. You're getting billed by the hour.

→ SOMEONE IN AD SALES

Flee. And we really shouldn't have to spell this one out.

→ CELEBRITY

Flee. STDs. Sorry, celebs! You look great, though. Nice teeth.

→ SNARKY BLOGGER

Fuck. It's good for a couple links.

---

* We are able to hear everything you think.

NAVIGATING THE SIX-COCKTAIL MEETING

WARNING!! WARNING!! THE SIX-COCKTAIL MEETING IS A TRAP.

BEWARE THE SIX-COCKTAIL MEETING. REPEAT: IT IS A TRAP.

AND NOW, GAWKER PRESENTS . . . THE SIX-COCKTAIL MEETING

COCKTAIL #1

I am me and you are you. I know things and you know things. We are two separate, high-security databases of insider knowledge.

COCKTAIL #2

You're funny! I'm funny. Hey, we actually like each other! Wow. We're enjoying this meeting.

COCKTAIL #3

You dated So-and-So? No FUCKING way!!!!! *I* dated So-and-So.

COCKTAIL #4

Did you guys do that wild thing together in bed? Isn't that crazy?!?!! I've never met anyone since then that can do that!!

COCKTAIL #5

Back to business: Here's every piece of privileged information you've ever wanted to know. Oh, and also . . . I don't like to talk shit . . . buuuuuuut . . . POO-POO KAKA POO-POO DOODIE, DOODIE, DOODIE, POO-POO DOO-DOO! KAKAPOOPOO DOODOO SHIT, SHIT, SHIT!

COCKTAIL #6

I can't believe a couple hours ago you were an enigma and today I'm crying with you at a diner at 5:00 a.m. Please, please get hit by a truck walking home. Please fall down a stairwell or slip in front of a cab. Oh, please be mugged and suffer a concussion or develop a few memory-impairing brain tumors. This never should have happened. But you kept pulling out your platinum card, didn't you? You kept sticking up your fat finger and saying "Another." I'll be jobless tomorrow. Was it worth it for a few (times 2) specialty cocktails? Absolutely not. Can I turn back time? Same answer. Are you a conniving city slickster with a high tolerance and a company card? Certainly. Was I duped? Again the answer is clear. I've sacrificed my career for a tab of roughly $60. If I am ever able to work again, I will venge myself upon thee with the utmost vengeance. For now . . .
I pass out with heavy heart.

SOLUTION: *Mocktails such as the Shirley Temple can save face and keep dignity intact.*

WHAT TO DO IF YOU'RE NOT A JEW AND YET WANT TO RUN THE MEDIA?

If you aren't Jewish and are female, you can marry a Jewish man. Your surname would become Jewish (something like Brillstein, Steinberg, or Cohen) and running some small fraction of the media would be an instantaneous result. Basically, the second you say "I do" you get a newspaper to run. Enjoy the Jewish lifestyle!

HELP! I GOT SO WASTED LAST NIGHT, I CAN BARELY BREATHE

Working hungover, i.e., "Friday at Every Office Across America," is a very common practice. Thursday nights are the new Friday nights and everyone's known it for years. You go out on a Thursday, you get a little buzz going, and you think: "You know what? I never have work to do on Fridays, I just download music. Why would I rush home to sleep when I'm having so much fun with vodka gimlets? It wouldn't make sense!"

And that's the logic that instructs you to keep staying out at a bar with your friends. In fact, "I'll be fine tomorrow" is the last thing you remember telling yourself. But when that AM radio commercial starts blasting out of your alarm clock, you begin to doubt your late-night philosophizing. An hour tardy, you're soon hobbling into the office with an ice pack in your hat. And there you sit: squinting under fluorescent lights, sleeping through a company meeting, and resting your head horizontally as you "read" an interoffice memo for a few hours. You're hungover at work.

Here are some tips for next time:

- Drink an Airborne tablet in water before you head out to the office. If you're a hippie, this translates into "Drink nettle tea." Both liquid solutions are packed with the vitamins you've pissed and sweated out in your extensive debauchery.

- Get a signed doctor's note that says you can leave early due to "hangover."

- Announce that you've joined AA, via megaphone.

- Become a "yes-man." It doesn't matter what you agree to, you can pick up the slack later when you have what is known as "mental capacity."

- Wear tennis attire and be like "I'm so beat from my tennis match!" No one could expect a drunk to play tennis in the wee hours before work, so you're all clear. And now your dried sweat, foul BO thing checks out, too.

RE-ORG JUST DESERTS*: HOW TO ACT WHEN YOU BECOME YOUR OLD BOSS'S BOSS

STOP

If you've followed the course set out for you in this book, tomorrow (or maybe even this afternoon) you'll be solidly situated within the ruling class. But beware: Today's intern is tomorrow's turbo-powered exec, today's exec is tomorrow's inmate, and so on. Re-orgs have become so commonplace, at this point they really should just be called orgs! (That's a great joke for the next time you have to deliver a speech at the office).

The upshot of this relative lack of positional security is that now, more than ever, every peon's wildest revenge fantasy is within reach. It's entirely within the realm of possibility that someone can become their own boss, while their boss is savagely demoted or fired.

If your superior is demoted, he or she will feel sore. You could wind up with an inefficient worker on your hands. No one wants a glum employee clouding their blue-sky thinking. It's up to you to use your management and leadership skills to put your ex-boss at ease. Under your rule, everyone's a winner.

Here are some behaviors that'll help smooth that rocky transition period and make a boss-cum-employee feel like a valued member of the team:

- Glide past your ex-boss and point winsomely: "I remember you!"

- Call your ex-boss "chief" or "chieftain" and salute often.

- Always be searching your ex-boss's eyes for tears with long, searching, unbroken eye contact, just in case it's been a hard day.

- Pout and say in baby talk: "I miss my old boss."

- Let your boss know that your chair is always open, should any feelings of nostalgia arise.

- To restore some sense of agency, let your old boss show you something. Like ask where the safe is located in your executive office.

* Yes, it is *deserts*, not *desserts*. Look it up.

AVOID INTERNSHIPS

Interning is historically unrewarding. It has always been so and shall always be so, as these excerpted letters from a Victorian-era intern illuminate:

August 14, 1881

Filing:

Mother and Father: You ask of my health. Today I find my finger quite badly sliced from filing. I am to complete this dreadful duty day after day—it is a load that never seems to lighten! One begins to wonder how a solitary company could even create so much information in need of filing, when very little of note ever seems to occur here.

Mental health:

My pulse is present . . . my heart continues with the characteristic ebb and flow that signifies the presence of precious life in mortal being . . . and yet I would like very much to die.

Do I think of you often? Of course. Not a moment passes when my life as a child isn't playing itself out in my mind like some glorious piece of theater. I see myself small, round, robust, running, happy, loved. Dancing or laughing or nibbling a cake in mother's arms, fatted by her milk... Today is a dark and different day. I sit in borrowed blazer and shoe, working to dawn's cruel light, declining all the social engagements this city has to offer ...

Lunch:

Dearest Mother and Father . . . I've been toiling for hours without any conceivable end in sight. I've had nothing to eat, no meal-break, while everyone else has meandered off to lunch engagements at the finest restaurants. They return rosy-cheeked with ales and ports in their blood . . . I am alone.

Flirtation:

There seems to be the prevailing impression that, as the youngest person within these hallowed walls, I am interested in constant attentions, from anyone who cares to practice upon me. I mean no injury to any party, but I have as yet to recognize in this office the face of a lover I would care to enchant. Yet at me they come, with wink and smile, with anecdote and "innocent" hand.

Friendship:

I made a friend once, but she has long since been fired.

Ambition:

Mother. Father. Presumably this internship is to serve as the gateway to future opportunity. I await even just a single one, and should it arrive … I would pounce upon it like a Tiger, with a fanged and vicious blood-thirst so animalistic in nature … I've allowed myself to digress. Back to sharpening pencils.

I shall take strength in the knowledge of your constant love, and think of you always.

—Anonymous Intern

Postscript, upon receipt of your letter in today's post:

Mother: I've snuck away to the supply closet to dash you off a quick note: I did receive the carrot bread and have been enjoying it for my lunches four days consecutive! Its taste is wondrous. It is nice to feel that a person cares for me in any sense of the word. I am lucky to have you. I must go! A conference has just ended!

Elaine's

■ An "Upper East Side staple," famously the stomping grounds of Tom Wolfe, Dominick Dunne, Lewis Lapham, Woody Allen, Nora Ephron, Candace Bushnell, and the list goes on. Regulars don't bother "describing the food" because they'd rather "not encourage business."

Swifty's

■ If you think "paying fifty dollars for a plate of pasta" makes it taste better, Swifty's "blend of uptown snobbery, ladies who lunch, and ladies who push lunch around their plates to make it look like they've eaten something" will be "up your alley."

Michael's

■ "Eyeballed entrances" and "obsequious waitstaff" sort of make up for "underwhelming" food and "tense" company. Media power players vie for privileged tables and "$30 salads" in a restaurant where seating is "more strategic than the current war effort."

Downtown Cipriani

■ "Fake tan town" is a great place for "ugly men with massive amounts of money" to wine and dine their "anorexic money grubber du jour." This is the epicenter where "pussy hounds and coin hounds collide" in a "passionate frenzy of ordering food they don't care about" and a plea to be seen.

Nobu

■ "Jay-Z and some Jews" plus assorted other notables enjoy "excellent food" at "morally offensive prices."

NYLA

■ (Ineligible. Closed three seconds after opening.)

Balthazar

■ "Model mommies," "Jersey spenders," and "French people" join forces at this hotspot of yesteryear cum tasty "rich people's late night diner."

Spotted Pig

■ Burgers "at full cow cost" grace the tables of this West Village, "haute bohemian" hangout. "Don't go to stalk": Celebs are whisked upstairs into privacy before you can "get a piece."

Algonquin Hotel

■ "Historic" legend famous for "round tables" and "barbed repartee" now comes off as "trying too hard." The "$10,000 martini" is a no-no for a power lunch, no matter how bad your potential partner/client/et cetera wants it. Prized staff of "Depends-able senior employees" serve the politicians, publishers, actors, and old people who cling to glory days when Parker and friends ruled the roost.

Soho House

■ "Just mention Nick Denton's name" at this "members only" Brit import and you should breeze past "snotty" front desk attendant— or be asked to "settle a tab."

KICK-ASS MEDIA CAREER MEDITATIONS

I MAKE IT HAPPEN.

I HAVE MORE CONTACTS.

I WORK OUT MORE REGULARLY.

I'M ON THE LIST.

I'M A BOLDFACED NAME.

MY ATTIRE IS THE SHARPEST IN EVERY ROOM.

NO MATTER WHAT, I HAVE THE BEST PERKS.

NO ONE IS MY EQUAL.

I STAND ALONE.

SERIOUSLY. SOMETIMES I FEEL REALLY, REALLY ALONE, EVEN THOUGH I KNOW PEOPLE LOOK UP TO ME AND THAT MY GOOGLE RESULTS ARE EXCEPTIONALLY STRONG. IT'S LIKE THE MORE SUCCESSFUL I GET (ON PAPER) THE MORE I UNDERSTAND THAT "ACHE OF LONELINESS" PEOPLE TALK ABOUT . . . *

* Published incomplete.

ACRONYM INSPIRATION

Cut 'n' tape! Perfect for your computer monitor, bulletin board, or company fridge.

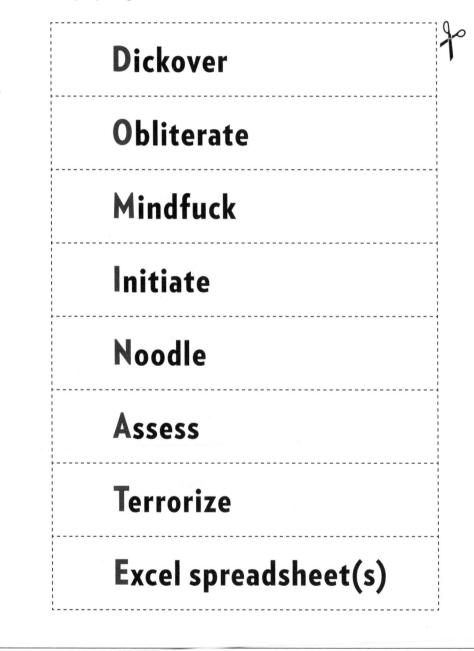

Dickover

Obliterate

Mindfuck

Initiate

Noodle

Assess

Terrorize

Excel spreadsheet(s)